MW00770353

James Callaway In The War Of 1812: Letters,

Diary And Rosters: Missouri Historical Society

Collections, October 1927

Edgar B. Wesley

VOLUME V.   October, 1927.   NUMBER 1.

MISSOURI HISTORICAL SOCIETY COLLECTIONS

· CONTENTS

HONORABLE DAVID ROWLAND FRANCIS. MEMORIAL
ADDRESS   .   .   .   .   *Hon. Harry B. Hawes*

GENEALOGICAL NOTES, RELATING TO THE ANCESTRY
OF DAVID ROWLAND FRANCIS AND HARRY
B. HAWES .   .   .   .   .   . *Breckinridge Jones*

THE VILLAGE UNDER THE HILL. A SKETCH OF
EARLY ST. LOUIS   .   .   . *Edward Villeré Papin*

JAMES CALLAWAY IN THE WAR OF 1812.
LETTERS, DIARY AND ROSTERS . *Edgar Bruce Wesley*

THE CALLAWAY FAMILY. FROM ORIGINAL RECORDS
Sarah Mercer Carpenter

NOTES AND QUERIES.

MISSOURI HISTORICAL SOCIETY
Jefferson Memorial
ST. LOUIS

David R Francis

DAVID ROWLAND FRANCIS*

By HON. HARRY B. HAWES,

United States Senator from Missouri.

It is not for me to attempt even a historical sketch of David Rowland Francis. This should be done by Walter B. Stevens, Walter Williams, or Collins Thompson, as soon as time wipes the tears from their eyes, so that they may do it clearly. My part is a mere picture, a small contribution, in this house of history, erected as a memorial to Thomas Jefferson.

I had for Governor Francis both admiration and regard. My mind is more upon the man than upon his achievements. My thought is for the rounded career, his many-sided human characteristics, his bigness, his absorbing personality, that drew to him all elements of society.

Let us visualize David Rowland Francis as he was before suffering from the blighting hand of foreign service.

There was never a finer picture of a real male man. No mollycoddle here, no sentimental theorist, no poser, no sycophant, no straddler, no hypocrite. He was a big man who had big conceptions, surrounded himself with big men and did big things. He had the vision for large things. He went to his objectives in a masterful way, sometimes with impatience, sometimes pushing aside without deference the obstacles that stood in his way. His designs were good and he gained his goal in straightforward combat.

---

* Memorial Address delivered, April 30, 1927, Louisiana Purchase Day, at the annual meeting of Missouri Historical Society in the Jefferson Memorial.

3

Gov. Francis enjoyed a cigar, a horse, a drink; delighted in a bright eye, a pretty face; responded to a good song, a good story, and a good friend. He served his friends, he served his city, he served his state, he served his nation with both ability and distinction. There is no taint or blemish upon his escutcheon. There is no ugly whisper or scandal left to scar his memory. He hit hard and took some good blows in return; and then reached out to help, to succor, to bind up wounds, to soften things and make life not only more pleasant but more honorable. He carried with him into adventures of great magnitude the heart of a boy. He saw the humorous, joyful things of life, and while demanding his full share, he was quick to divide his pleasures with others.

David Francis was a fighter when as a boy he crawled on a coach and sold papers during the war in a small Kentucky town. He was a fighter when in the closing years of his life he faced a mob in a foreign city and, with pistol in hand, defended the ancient "right of castle."

Can't you see him now as on Hospital Saturday, with some chosen friends, he visits the booths in the hotels and office buildings, covered with badges, smiling, joking, the picture of health, good spirits, and the very embodiment of good fellowship, the leader, the inspiration of our most popular charity? How many will remember the old days at the Den in the Merchants Exchange, during the Veiled Prophet's Ball, when he led in the Queen and, in his inimitable way, made another queen of each maid and each matron?

How he spread sunshine and good fellowship! He knew by first name more men than any other man in the city, and more men knew him and called him "Dave." The "Dave" was not a familiarity; it was esteem, regard and affection. When the ball game was opened he was there; when a school was dedicated he spoke; when a park was opened he presided; when a new Union Station was needed, he led the way; when a bridge was required, he made the plan. He built the very hall in which we are assembled tonight.

In affairs of a city, as in the life of an individual, there comes a time when a forward step must be taken, or the ground already gained will be lost. This period came when the people made Rolla Wells mayor, and with that came the inspiration for the World's Fair and the inspiration and organization came from David Francis.

I will not detain you with an extended discussion of that event. Suffice to say he invited the nation and the nation came; he invited the world and the world came. They came from the farms and they came from the small towns, and they came from the factories and from the colleges of learning. They visited our city and they liked it. They found it was a city of homes, of generous impulse, of fine old traditions; a place good to live in, to grow up in, and in which to be buried. They came from the four quarters of the nation to the heart of the nation. They saw the possibilities of trade and commerce. The forward stride which we took then was necessary. It was not a mere plan of advertising, it was an awakening of the spirit of the city to do better things. It kept St. Louis moving forward when she might have stood still. Our progress today may be attributed largely to the inspiration of Francis and the wonderful group of patriotic men who surrounded him and united with him in this great enterprise.

David Francis had the graces of the courtly Jefferson. He, like Jefferson, was fond of music, of the dance, of literature, fine paintings, fine horses, courageous men and amiable women. He liked children and the children all loved him.

Francis helped Grover Cleveland and supported

him in office for eight years. He helped Rolla Wells and supported him for eight years. He helped Woodrow Wilson and supported him for eight years. But each president was his president; each governor was his governor; each mayor was his mayor. He believed in orderly government and sustained the office even though he did not approve the man.

Twenty-five years ago the Kentucky Society of St. Louis attended a homecoming celebration in that state. We visited Lexington, where the finest horses were exhibited for our inspection. I remember a great chestnut stallion, with delicate nostrils, small ears, arched neck, long mane and flowing tail held high. He, by the way, was named "Governor Francis." They brought him out. The Governor stroked his nose; he felt his fetlocks; he passed his hand over his glossy mane and the magnificient animal remained perfectly docile, seeming to sense the fact that he was being handled by a friend. A few minutes later another member of the party approached. The great stallion rose in the air, whirled, came down to the ground and kicked; giving his colored attendant much trouble in holding him. The Governor stepped quickly to his aid, and the magnificent animal came to attention. I watched the Governor with great interest on this occasion. His expression of keen appreciation, his distress at the display of bad temper, his gratification when the temper had passed, and the splendid animal had recovered his poise; the whole incident in fact was characteristic of the man.

Later, on this same trip, we attended the trial of Howard, a mountaineer charged with killing Governor Goebel. As we entered the courtroom a deputy sheriff stood guard at the door. The Governor was first in line. The deputy politely asked him if he carried a gun. For a moment there was indecision in the Governor's face. Then he smiled. The deputy sheriff said: "Governor, we will check your gun, put it in this barrel and I will return it as you leave the courtroom.'' He made the same inquiry of each member of our party. None made a deposit. I looked in the barrel as we passed by, and the bottom was covered with revolvers, each one bearing a tag with the owner's name.

Returning to the hotel, the courthouse incident brought on a discussion of old Kentucky feuds, fights and duels. Joined by some of the ''Kentucky Colonels,'' the stories went back to the Indian days, of the frontier adventures, of Aaron Burr on the Ohio river, of the War of 1812, when Kentucky riflemen (amongst whom was one of Francis's ancestors) took the long march to support ''Old Hickory'' at the Battle of New Orleans, of the Black Hawk war, in which the frontiersmen held their cabins for an advancing civilization; of the Mexican war, and of the Civil War, in which Kentucky's sons divided. Some one told the Governor the amusing story of my grandfather, Richard Hawes, whose inauguration as Confederate Governor of the state was interrupted by Buell's artillery; how he finished his speech and rode out of the Capital on a mule, shelled by advancing troops, with his speech and state papers in his hat.

This Kentucky history formed the background of the Governor's life. He carried it with him in his association with men, in business, in charity, in executive office, and in diplomacy. It was the bold, assertive, determined quality of the frontiersman which had been transplanted into his being and moved his stalwart figure in the front rank of every occupation. He was of Scotch-Irish ancestry, descended from the men who fought for liberty, for tolerance, for local government in the crags and mountains of Scotland. He was a figure like that of Robert Bruce.

We all remember the long and destructive filibuster

at the close of the last session of Congress, led by
Senator David Reed, of Pennsylvania. Our senior
Senator, Reed of Missouri, was trying to break the
filibuster and secure a vote. These two senators are
distant cousins, both Scotch-Irish. In the cloakroom
one evening, a tired senator was complaining of the
futility and wåste of time in the contest. Some one
referred to the relationship. Another said: ''They
are both Scotch-Irish; what can you expect?'' And
one of the auditors, turning away, said: ''They may
be both Scotch-Irish, but for the last week it has
been more Irish than Scotch.'' And so it was with
the Governor. Sometimes in fighting mood, the
Irish was on top, and sometimes the shrewdness of
the Scotchman prevailed, and when the two com-
bined, it made the combination which has left its
impress throughout America.

When young David Francis first came to St. Louis,
he founded his career on the old Merchants
Exchange. That was the period when steamboats
lined our wharves, when the Merchants Exchange was
the heart and center of every activity in St. Louis.
It was the place where the Veiled Prophet's Ball was
born; where great public movements were inspired;
from which came Seth Cobb, Governor Stanard, and
men who contributed to our civic and state development.

On its floor each day there were miniature battles.
They were gained by quick decision, by a strong
voice, by a hand raised quickly, by an offer, or a
trade, by a bargain, which men made without paper
or signed agreement. It was one man's word given
to another. It required quick thought, quick action,
quick decision, and this early training was respon-
sible for many of the dominant traits of leadership
in Francis.

As president of the Merchants Exchange he quickly
attracted city-wide attention. He was made mayor

of the city. As mayor he grew in popularity in the state and, surrounded by a small coterie of loyal friends, the early political days of Francis, associated with Rolla Wells, Breckinridge Jones, Charley Maffitt, and Fred Zeibig, formed a group of big, patriotic business men who did things, and while attending to business and social engagements they made real contributions to political advancement.

Francis attended the wedding; he kissed and danced with the bride; he sent the silver spoon or cup to the baby; he acted as pallbearer and followed the friend's body to the grave; he seemed to have time in the midst of a busy career to do these human things and become the best known man in St. Louis. Travel where you might in any part of the world, and the query was, "How is Governor Francis?" His personality had carried far beyond the confines of his own state. In distant lands, wherever men travel, they knew the big Missourian. He was a "round table" man and, while fond of talking, he had the fine faculty of making other men talk.

Rarely did he go alone. He loved companionship. When he moved or visited, he was usually in company with two or three companions. He drew attention and held it; made other people do things under his inspiration who were unaware of the fact that he had caused them to act. He was proud of what he called his "thirty-six feet of sons." These six sons were selected to carry the father and chieftain to his grave.

As mayor of St. Louis Francis gave a business administration. He paved the city, reduced the rate of interest paid on the public debt, bought the site for the new waterworks at the Chain of Rocks, reduced the cost of gas, and forced a great railroad corporation to pay a million dollars into the city treasury. As governor he attracted national attention by the vigor of his administration. He was a new kind of governor for that day. Putting business methods into operation, he resurrected and put the National Guard upon a permanent basis, passed the Australian ballot system, created a school-book commission and uniform textbooks, created a geological survey, established stable state finances, and followed the same course he pursued as mayor with industry and administrative understanding. He reorganized the State University, created an endowment fund and popularized that institution. As Secretary of the Interior he studied the problems of the West. His long and intimate knowledge of the farmer and grain was helpful.

Governor Francis liked the "big outdoors," and had as his field assistant, William Zevely, a devoted follower and indefatigable worker of the same warm and genial character as the Governor. During both administrations of Grover Cleveland, Francis was his close friend and political adviser. Their contact was intimate, and the great New Yorker relied upon his judgment in making political appointments.

He was sent as a delegate to the Baltimore Convention in support of Missouri's favorite candidate, Champ Clark. He helped organize the convention; was one of the floor leaders who saw Champ Clark's lead reach a majority. Later he gave his tireless energy in support of Woodrow Wilson, and his popularity, wide acquaintance, and reputation as a substantial business man, was of inestimable help in both the Wilson elections.

Although in very poor physical condition, Gov. Francis attended the last Democratic Convention in New York, and was an interested spectator during its long struggle. While ill health prevented active participation, he followed the fortunes of the Jeffersonian party with interest and enthusiasm to the end.

It was the followers of Jefferson who made Francis

mayor. It was the followers of Jefferson who elected him governor. It was a student of Jefferson who placed him in his Cabinet; and it was a real disciple of Jefferson who appointed him ambassador. How appropriate then, in this Memorial of Jefferson, is a discussion of the man whose distinctions in life came from the supporters of Jefferson. He was never offensive in his partisanship and, while he kept his party's faith, he retained as well his personal friends. When he accepted his last political assignment he was three score and five. Far-seeing men at that time knew we could not long remain out of the struggle; the whole world was at war.

One of the scenes of greatest tragedy was in Russia, the country to which he was assigned. Its borders had been drenched in blood; its civil government was dead; it was a scene not only of civil decay and war, but it was the center for schemers and plotters of all nations. It was the spot where men of various nationalities were trying to destroy not only the bodies of men, but their minds. It was there that the great battle of propaganda was fought.

Governor Francis went not only courageously but blithely to his post of danger. It was his last call for public service, and he answered it. He left his family, and his business to the management of his sons, at a period when the perplexities and uncertainties of the time demanded his personal presence to preserve the fortune which he had built up during years of struggle. I remember his words, the fire and emphasis of his departing speech, in his farewell to his fellow townsmen:

"If my government, in its wisdom, calls me to an important post, which it thinks I am competent to fill on account of my years or my experience in domestic government, or in national or international commerce, I would be a poor citizen indeed if I permitted personal interests, or friendly associations, or love of ease, or even ties of consanguinity, to interfere or to prevent a favorable response on my part.

"Fear of jeopardizing whatever of reputation I may have gained in public affairs or in commerce is not one of my guides of action. If it were, I should be a coward, and unworthy of the respect of my fellows."

This was the Francis spirit. He went upon his duty and his duty brought his death. He accepted a position with nothing but hardship ahead, physical danger and diplomatic uncertainty. The careful politician would have refused. The cautious diplomat would have declined. It was not a place in which to seek honor or publicity: It was an assignment of hard, dangerous, thankless work.

Francis's contribution to American history will be written later, but even now we know it will be a chapter of American courage. I was in Spain when a number of those who were attached to his embassy in Russia arrived. They sought me to tell of their admiration and love for their Chief, especially for his courage in demanding respect for Americans. In listening to their praise, I felt a reflected glory as a fellow-citizen and a friend.

We remember the attack of the mob upon the American Embassy in Russia. Our ambassador sent the faithful Phil for his gun. "Stop," commanded the ambassador, facing the mob. "This is not Russian, it is American territory; you cannot put your foot in here!" But the mob pushed forward. Again he said: "This is American territory. I will kill the first man that crosses the threshold!" The mob wavered. He displayed his weapon and the mob broke and went away.

No marines were there for Francis; no policemen. With his own revolver he stopped the mob. It was the fine old spirit of the frontier. It was part of the best traditions of Kentucky and Missouri. At that time he was not an ambassador; he was the frontiersman guarding the sacred threshold! When St. Louis erects the statue to the ambassador, I would have it a reproduction of this scene in the land of the Czar and the Bolshevik. Francis on the threshold of an American domicile; Francis saying, ''This is American territory. I will kill the first man that crosses the threshold!''

Had he lived in the days of Scottish feuds, he would have wielded a broad-axe or twanged a giant bow. Had he lived during the Crusades, he would have straddled a horse, and with vizor down charged the Infidel. Had he lived during the Revolution, he would have been one of the ragged soldiers who followed the tattered flag of Washington. He would have shouldered a rifle and followed Andrew Jackson to the Battle of New Orleans. These were not his times. But he was part of the World War, and the last American to leave that living hell of carnage, rapine and human slaughter. When government disappeared and torch and bomb struck and destroyed one of the oldest governments in the world, he sent his secretaries and all of his attaches first, then followed last, with his faithful colored man.

The Governor loved his country and would have sacrificed and fought for it at any period of its history. He was that kind of man. Just a few days before the Armistice was declared, our ambassador was carried by sailors on board ship at Archangel. This closed three years of service in a distracted country, and was the beginning of the physical end. Even his great frame at his age could not stand the strain. But the break did not come until his full duty had been performed.

It must be remembered that Governor Francis never lost faith in the great body of the Russian people, and predicted that time would bring a stable and sane government. And he desired to live that he might assist in the coming rehabilitation. Upon his return home, one of our famous quartettes composed and sang a song. It was not classical, but it was the feeling of St. Louis then, and the city is of the same opinion now.

"He's a roving son of Liberty, our townsman and our Dave;
He saw the old red terror where the Czar went to his grave;
But he stayed right there on duty when a man must needs be brave;
    And we're proud to get him back to old Missouri.
"He's one of the war's great heroes, our own big native son;
He was there for Uncle Samuel when he needed things well done;
He held the fort in Petrograd, and didn't know how to run;
    And he's mighty welcome back to old Missouri."

Governor Francis gave his old mansion, the scene of World's Fair festivities, the meeting-place of business leaders and statesmen, to the Boy Scouts and the Junior Chamber of Commerce. He gave a park to St. Louis, a drinking-fountain to Missouri University, and gave freely of his heart and brain for everything that went to make a better city and a greater state.

The Governor enjoyed a story; he told good ones himself. He led the laugh; his was the hand that first applauded. He said the helpful word and slapped the back in approval. He was a gracious host and an appreciative guest. Always the leader; in civics, in society, in business, in politics, in sport, David Francis was first. As one of our papers editorially expressed it, he was "our most distinguished St. Louisian".

Let us think of David Rowland Francis frequently; call up his recollection often, and in this, the Memorial he erected and named for Jefferson, keep a special place for him and the story of the part he played in the growth of our city, in the development of our state, in the national halls at Washington, and in the foreign land in which he exhibited the frontier spirit of Kentucky and Missouri.

GENEALOGICAL NOTES, RELATING TO THE ANCESTRY
OF DAVID ROWLAND FRANCIS AND
HARRY B. HAWES

Given by Breckinridge Jones, First Vice-President of the Missouri
Historical Society when introducing Senator Hawes
for the foregoing oration.

DAVID ROWLAND FRANCIS
(Showing descent from Colonel Richard Callaway.)

COLONEL RICHARD CALLAWAY m   FRANCES WALTON
about 1724-1780.
Killed by Indians. (*Revolution
on Upper Ohio, Frontier of Virginia*, by Thawaites and Kel-
logg.)
Collins, Hist. of Ky. Vol. 2, p.
110.

CHRISTOPHER IRVINE   m   LYDIA CALLAWAY
11 Sept. 1755-Oct. 6, 1786. Killed
by Indians in Ohio.

THOMAS ROWLAND   m   FRANCES IRVINE

DAVID IRVINE ROWLAND   m   MAHALA TYREE
1800—1863.   1829   1800—1868.

JOHN BROADDUS FRANCIS   m   ELIZA C. ROWLAND
1819—1894.   1830—1898

DAVID ROWLAND FRANCIS   m   JANE PERRY
1st Oct. 1850—   d of John D. Perry
15th Jan. 1927.

Christopher Irvine, born September 11, 1755, moved to Kentucky
in 1778, Madison county, and established Irvine Station. Married
Lydia Callaway, daughter of Colonel Richard Callaway. Fought
against the British and Indians; was a member of the Convention
that met at Danville in 1785; killed by Indians in Ohio about
Oct. 6, 1786. (*The Irvines and their Kin*, p. 156.)
Richard Callaway was born in Caroline County, Virginia, about
the year 1724: When 16 years of age he removed to what became
Bedford County, East of the Peaks of Otter. During the French
and Indian Wars, he was Capt. of Militia and afterwards attained
the rank of Colonel. He first accompanied Boone to Kentucky in
the spring of 1775 and in the autumn brought his family to Boonesborough. The following summer his two daughters were captured
by Indians but were later rescued.
Col. Callaway was representative for Kentucky County in 1777—
Justice of the Peace and participant in the big siege of Boonesborough. In 1779, he was chosen trustee of the town and commissioned to open a ferry. In preparing the ferry boat he was shot
and instantly killed by the Indians March 8, 1780.—*Revolution on
Upper Ohio, Frontiers of Virginia*, by Thwaites.

HARRY BARTOW HAWES

JOHN CARTER	m	SARAH LUDLOW
b. in England; moved to Corotoman, in Lancaster Co. Va., in 1649; buried there in 1669:		a grand dau. of Roger Ludlow, Gov. of Mass., one of the numerous descendants of Isabel de Vermandois from whom came the following Presidents of the U. S.: George Washington, John Adams, John Quincy Adams, Thomas J e ff e r s o n, William Henry Harrison, Abraham Lincoln, U. S. Grant, Grover Cleveland. Benj. Harrison, Theodore Roosevelt. (See The Scientific Monthly, Dec. 1921, article by Dr. David Starr Jordan.)

ROBERT CARTER	m 1688	JUDITH ARMISTEAD 1665-1699
of Corotoman, 1668-1732, known as "King Carter." (No early Virginian had so many distinguished descendants, conspicuous among them being Robert E. Lee.		

DR. GEORGE NICOLAS	m	ELIZABETH CARTER
		Her sister Judith, m. Mann Page of Rosedale 1698-1730. Their son Mann Page was member Congress in 1777 m. Alice Grymes and their son was Gov. of Va. 1802.
		Her half sister Anne m. Benj. Harrison of Berkeley whose son was Benj. Harrison, signer of Declaration of Independence, and Governor of Virginia; his son President of the U. S. 1841, and his grandson also President of U. S. 1888.

ROBERT CARTER NICOLAS	m	ANN CARY
Burgess, Member Colonial Council and Treasurer of the Colony of Va.		of distinguished Virginia family.

GEORGE NICOLAS   m   MARY SMITH

one of Jefferson's staunchest and most efficient friends. The First Attorney General of Kentucky. Nicholas County, Ky. named for him. Said to have written "The Kentucky Resolutions of 1798." His brother, Wilson Cary Nicholas, was U. S. Senator from Va.

No Virginia family contributed more to Mr. Jefferson's personal success than the powerful family of Nicholases—powerful in talents, powerful in probity, powerful in their numbers and their union. On every page of Mr. Jefferson's political history, the names of George, John, Wilson Cary, and Philip Norborne Nicholas, are conspicuous.

(Collins), Hist. of Ky. Vol. 2, p. 663.)

(Randall's Life of Thomas Jefferson, Vol. 1, p. 360.)

(Beveridge's Life of John Marshall.)

dau. of Samuel Smith, Member of Cabinet of both Presidents Jefferson and Madison, U. S. Senator and Gov. of Maryland.

RICHARD HAWES   m   HENRIETTA MORRISON NICOLAS
1818

Member of Congress from Ashland district, commanded Company in Black Hawk War. Confederate Governor of Ky.

(See Collins' History of Ky. Vol. 2, p. 81.)

(Biographical Encyclopedia of Ky. p. 142.)

the 12th child of Col. George Nicolas.

SMITH NICOLAS HAWES   m   SUSAN ELIZABETH SIMRALL

(His brother, Morrison Hawes, was Brig. Genl. C. S. A.)

HARRY BARTOW HAWES   m   ELIZABETH EPPES OSBORNE ROBINSON

U. S. Senator from Missouri. Five of his g. g. grandfathers served under Washington.

Buried in the cemetery at Monticello, the home of Jefferson, are fourteen of the families of Senator and Mrs. Hawes.

Whose Va. ancestry was alike notable. Among her ancestors was William Branch Giles, U. S. Senator and Governor of Va.

(See Bowers "Jefferson & Hamilton.")

(National Cyclopedia of American Biography, Vol. 15, p. 448.)

THE VILLAGE UNDER THE HILL

A Sketch of Early St. Louis.[1]

By EDWARD VILLERE PAPIN.

The devastating march of modernism had not cast its blight on St. Louis in the year 1785. The settlement that then surrounded Laclede's trading post had taken on the dimensions and dignity of a village, a very beautiful village, and for the most part a peaceful one, that stretched its length along the bluff by the waterside.

This bluff was not like the tall cliffs that one notices from the decks of steamboats on the upper Mississippi, but of moderate height, rising some thirty to fifty feet from the water's edge, enough to save the houses from flood without denying easy access to the river.

Westwardly, behind the houses and the barns that stood back of them, the ground rose again gradually, so that the evening shadows of the neighboring woods fell early on the village, whence it came that St. Louis was sometimes called "The Village under the Hill."

Now in 1785, at which date it has been endeavored to center this sketch, the village had attained a certain dignity, a position among villages, for in that year it passed from its infancy and became of age. Aye, one might say that it came into its prime, for ere the lapse of a like period it was fated to cease, as such, and with a larger population, under a different flag, and ruled by a new people, to commence the achievement of that destiny as a great city foreseen by its founder.

But in the day of which we write much had yet to happen. France was still a kingdom; Louisana, a

1 Compiled principally from the notes of the late Pierre Chouteau.

Spanish colony; and St. Louis, a French settlement under Spanish rule, the prettiest village in the Mississippi Valley.

If we visit the site of the old town, it will tax the mind to reconstruct a picture of things as they were. In many of the cities of the Eastern seaboard, begun over a century earlier, there stand, as monuments to the fine civilization of their time, houses that are copied but not excelled by the best builders of our day. St. Louis had such in its infancy, but, as with almost every other city of the United States that has achieved greatness, with a few notable exceptions, they have gone down before the march of what is called Progress.

Gray and time-worn buildings on the river front now cast their shadows where cot and mansion once adorned the hillside. Not a trace remains of the town, save the river that flows by the ancient site, and the hills, in so far as they have been spared, that still rise, as far as their former limits.

The bluff is gone, but it is still steep climbing from the levee to the site of the old fort at Fourth and Walnut Streets.

Sudden Growth

St. Louis differed from many of the settlements in this, that its first growth was not a gradual one. Its foundation coincided with the passing of the territory east of the river from French to English rule, in consequence of which many of the colonists in the river towns on that side were easily persuaded by Laclede to throw their fortunes with his own, at *San Luis des Illinois,* as it was also called. So they came, a population long past the pioneer stage of development, consolidating their settlements into one village where they made themselves new homes. There, in contrast to some of the phases of life in later years, they lived undisturbed by the passage of steamboats, or the arrival of railway trains, by the eccentricities of sophisticated legislatures, or by unwarranted federal encroachments; hardy and intelligent, they strove to make the most of themselves and of their local resources, which were rich and unlimited.

There came but little change in these first twenty-one years. The village extended along the river front from what is now Poplar Street on the south, to Franklin Avenue on the North, and westwardly as far as Fourth Street. But this latter street did not then exist, nor for fifty years afterwards. The line of fortifications, projected and partially completed by Colonel Auguste Chouteau, reached the crest of the rise, where that street now runs, but, in the original town as laid out by Laclede in 1764, there were but the three long streets, running approximately north and south, that paralleled the river and with their cross streets, virtually as today, enclosed some forty-nine blocks. Main Street was then the *Rue Royale;* Second Street, the *Rue de l'Eglise;* and Third Street, *Rue des Granges.* Of the cross streets, there were but two that reached the river front, Walnut and Morgan. The others, because of the bluff, stopped at Main Street.

The slope on which the village stood was not as gradual as it is today, and the walking within its confines is described as being tiring for any but an active person. The ascent from the river at Walnut was steep, a climb of around fifty feet to the level of Main. Between Main and Second Streets the ground lay fairly level, although between Chestnut and Vine there was a hollow, which in wet weather was filled with water to a depth of several feet. There was a marshy pond at Fourth Street and Washington Avenue where one could fish, and where there was some duck shooting in the spring and fall. The highest ground was at the fort, at Fourth

Street, whence the slope was gradual in a south-
easterly direction to the river at Poplar. So much
for the early plan and topography of St. Louis.
Should one seek a better understanding, let him visit
one of the high lying up-river towns. He will find
one where the grader and paver have not had their
way, and there prove to his satisfaction that the
going underfoot, in the early days, must have exacted
exertion sufficient to enhance the hardiness of the
inhabitants.

The village has been spoken of as usually peaceful.
So it always was, as far as its inhabitants could
make it so. Only once was there serious disturbance, when in 1780 the hitherto distant drums
of the American Revolution sounded loudly at its
very outskirts. At British instigation the settlement
was attacked by Indians, and although no entrance
was effected into the town itself, their repulse was
not accomplished without loss of life. Until that
year, St. Louis had been an open village, as unde-
fended then, as is the city today. Following this peril,
Colonel Chouteau, whose military abilities were of
no mean order, undertook its fortification. His plan,
as projected, shows the town girdled on the land
sides with a well conceived line of stockade, so
designed as to insure an effective cross fire in the
event of assault. The main salients were strengthened by three Martello towers, large round stone
block houses with sloping roofs. One stood to the
north of the town, at or near the stockade; another,
the principal one, sometimes called the Fort, at the
center of the western boundary; while the third
guarded the southern approach.

The stockade was never completed, if indeed it
ever consisted of more than a palisade surrounding
the central tower, as is shown in some early
drawings. Fortunately, there was never again
occasion to man the village outworks. It prospered

peacefully, grew into a city, and so endured for
many years before the tide of war again menaced it,
in 1861, when its destiny was determined by the
coup d'état, sometimes known as the "Affair at Camp
Jackson."

STYLE OF ARCHITECTURE

Because of the destruction of every structure in
the original village, wonder arises concerning the
habitations of our forefathers. Not an example of
their building remains, but there are pictures,
drawings, and a few paintings, made then or shortly
thereafter, that give us a fair idea of their dwellings. These were scattered fairly evenly along the
forty-nine blocks of the settlement. We read in
Billon's *Annals,* that a few years earlier there were
some hundred houses of wood and about fifteen of
stone. They faced for the most part on what are
now Main and Second Streets; Third Street, as the
original name suggests, was used for their barns
and granaries. The land beyond, to the line of fortifications, was given over to pasturage.

The space bounded by Market and Walnut Streets,
and from the Fort on the hill down to the river's
bank, was the heart and center of the settlement.

That plot where the old Cathedral stands was dedicated to church purposes from the beginning, but in
the first days of the colony the church which was
built of logs faced eastwardly on Second Street.
Near it stood the parish house, and behind and
around them lay the graveyard.

Eastwardly again, the land between these streets
was occupied at first by Laclede, and in after years
by Colonel Auguste Chouteau, whose extensive stone
manor, with its gardens and slave quarters covered
the entire square. The last block of all, running from
main Street to the river, was open and was known
as the *Place Publique* or Market Place.

AUGUSTE CHOUTEAU MANSION

The houses of the greater number of the *habitants,* were made of logs, somewhat like those one yet sees in remote places, but differing in this, that the timbers instead of being laid crib fashion, horizontally, were placed on end. An interesting example of this kind of building can be seen, unless it has been recently removed, in a house used for parish purposes near the church in Cahokia. Although sheathed with boards on the outside, the structure of vertical logs remains uncovered in portions of the interior. Such houses were small, containing from one to three rooms, and were usually whitewashed on the outside. The better class of dwellings were of stone, quarried from the bluffs. They were spacious and well built, walnut and mahogany being freely used in the interiors, while the stone work was skillfully dressed and cemented. Their sloping roofs often overhung, covering broad verandas, and supported by tall columns. These verandas were commonly a full story above the ground and were reached by steps, as can be still seen in many old houses in Louisiana. Underneath was the so called cellar or basement, wherein were the store rooms, and infrequently, the kitchen. Their plan was simple, a large hall or living room in the center into which all other rooms opened. This, the family's room, was indeed a living room for them in a sense that is now hardly understood. In our times the family, as such, because of changed conditions of living, does not enjoy that unity so characteristic of Old World traditions, such as survived in Louisiana as long as it remained a province. And there were families in those days. Custom had not yet ruled that two children were enough, and the baptismal records of the French colonies give ample justification for the lack of encouragement to immigration. It wasn't needed.

After the living room the next in size and

importance was the dining room. Besides the table itself, of vastness sufficient for the family, there were two ample serving tables which in emergency could be added thereto, so extending the board and the hospitality of the house so as to care for all comers. The kitchen differed in arrangement and location from that of today. Seldom adjoining the dining room it was not infrequenty in a separate building, the service between being maintained by the younger negro servants. On occasions of entertainment there could be seen a line of these youngsters passing swiftly to the dining room, laden with the generous output of the cook house. And there, in the kitchen a kingdom apart, ruled in majesty less only than that of her mistress, the aged negro cook. At her frown her junior satellites quailed, and at her bidding they came and went with a fervor that would gladden the heart of a housewife today. Under her benevolent despotism the young girls helped in the kitchen and became themselves cooks in due time. The boys learned obedience and respect for their elders, while they kept up the service of supply between kitchen and house.

From the hewn rafters of the room hung ropes of onions, of garlic, of red peppers and of delicious morelles. The walls were lined with cupboards and tables at which the work of preparation was carried on. It is suggested that in such a kitchen there must have been embarrassment for lack of modern appliances and that the methods employed were too primitive to be good. It may be so, or rather it might have been, had the responsibility fallen upon an operative graduated from a modern school of domestic science, for lack of such our forbears would have been grateful had they but known. As it was, they enjoyed their turkeys, roasted as is possible only on a spit before the open fire; and omelettes, manipulated at just the right height above the glowing embers. But the *batterie de cuisine,* as it was called, had other implements besides spit and frying pan. If there was no electric range, there was a fire place, cavernous and vast, flanked by great iron cranes. Innumerable pots, pans, and dutch ovens were at hand, while before the blazing logs rose high and-irons, crossed with a heavy bar from which depended kettles, stew pots, and roasting game. The fire was enlivened with an ample bellows, while before it, armed with a long cooking spoon ministered the cook, high priestess of an art now wellnigh forgotten. In many of the minor operations of the kitchen, hands and feet must needs serve for what is now accomplished by an organization and fewer servants. The essential difference lay in this, that with few facilities and primitive appliances, kitchen administration demanded the generous use of brains, which accounts perhaps for the more satisfactory results. But there were lacking many resources that one forgets today because they are forever at hand. There were no corner groceries. Staple things like sugar and salt had to be brought from far away New Orleans. They came in barges, hauled painfully by hand, save where a favoring wind helped stem the swift current of the river. The way was long and the shipments infrequent, for it took three months for the keel boats, as they were called, to make the passage. Indeed, certain supplies arrived but once during the year. Wherefore the store room, and this was *not* within the jurisdiction of the cook. Far from it, and far be it from the enforced thriftiness of the mistress of the house to delegate the keeping of the keys. The efficiency of the negro cook lay in the use rather than in the conservation of supplies, for, like all of her kind, even to this day, she had an abiding faith in the plenteousness of "More where that came from." In this, and in other limitless details, lay the cares of the housewife, to whom the servants looked, not alone as ultimate authority, but for help in time of trouble, for care in days of sickness, and for kindly sympathy at all times.

The very safety of the household required a rigid administration of supplies, which she measured and distributed each day to those who used them. One section of the store room, partitioned from the rest, contained the family store of wines and liquors, which then as now, in civilized communities, were deemed an essential accessory to the table.

MUNICIPAL PROBLEMS

If the town was not adorned with those urban blessings, steel houses, sidewalks of granitoid, and streets of nice black asphaltum, there were compensations from which, in their ignorance, the inhabitants derived rare pleasure. For example, they did not have to plant trees. These overgrew the slopes on which the village stood in all the glory of the Missouri woodland. For many years the streets and the gardens about the houses, were shaded and adorned with a wealth of oak, maple, walnut, elm, and hickory, the like of which is now unknown in any city of our country. Besides these, there were cultivated fruit trees and flowers, and within the walled enclosures of the greater houses, there were gardens, very beautiful to see through the long summers, while, in its duly appointed place, beyond the orchard, there was found, as in France to this day, the *potager,* or vegetable garden.

The need of water works was not realized in the beginning, and the quantity of water available for household purposes was limited. Every gallon used, save only for the laundry, was carried up from the river. The process was picturesque, if inconvenient. Under the direction of the oldest and most dependable of the negro servants, the water casks, mounted on wheels, were hauled by horses or oxen to the river's edge, filled, and on their return emptied into large unglazed earthern jars, brought from New Orleans for the purpose. Therein the mud settled to the bottom, while the slow evaporation from the porous surface cooled the contents sufficiently to make it palatable. This was before the days when it became necessary to clean our water supply with chemicals, for at that time there were no settlements upstream to befoul it. Taken as it came, it was somewhat rich in flavor, as well as in color, and there are those who stoutly contend that no water on earth can compare with that of the Mississippi, *au naturel*.

Domestic Equipment

The family laundry did not depend upon the river, but was taken care of at Mill Creek, then called *La Petite Rivière*. Wash day was an institution, and each Monday morning there moved a long file of negro women, laden with *panniers,* carried by some on their heads, nicely balanced; by others, in little push carts. The work was done in cabins by the water's edge, or on platforms built out over the stream, where advantage could be had of the running water. Instead of clothes lines, the bushes served very nicely, and the work went on to the accompaniment of songs and laughter, interrupted only for exchange of gossip concerning their respective families.

The furniture that filled the houses varied from the output of the village carpenter shop, to the finest pieces of rosewood and San Domingo mahogany brought from New Orleans, the West Indies, and even from France. While not abundant, there remains enough of this early furniture to evidence that the residents of Upper Louisiana were not barred by their isolation from providing themselves with furnishings that compared favorably with those in use in the English colonies. Their supply of the finer woods was, perhaps, even more abundant, for one seldom sees furniture, of that era, that can compare for richness of material, with the few rarely beautiful specimens that have come down to us from colonial St. Louis.

The decoration of this work was perhaps more fanciful than is found in the graceful patterns of old and New England. Indeed, its beauty depended largely on carved adornment, which suggests that the artists, rather than use the design of others, sought to reproduce in wood (even as did those who wrought in stone in the Gothic ages) the marvels of foliage and fruit and flower that abounded in the land where they were made.

In the first years, the efforts, even of the leaders in the colony, had been confined to the struggle for maintenance. As the excess fruits of their labors accumulated, and they learned from those newly-come sojourners from the outer world, the officers of the Spanish garrison, that their furs could be transmuted into luxuries, furniture and plate, and fine linens, the waterways leading hither became presently freighted with many a barge, carrying rich cargoes from New Orleans, from Canada, and from France.

Problems and Economics

There were households to be cared for in those forgotten days, and therein the women found their occupation. It was a necessary care but they did it with right good will, for was not the home their domain where each housewife was mistress of all? And nobly did they answer to that happy obligation. Although it is long past a hundred years since the village housewives ministered and ruled, the traditions of themselves and of their work are cherished today as the dearest heritage of their descendants. If the husband was the provider, the wife administered the fruits of his labor, for it was an equal partnership. Besides the household budget and the work of administration, to her ever came the first appeal for sympathy, and the final demand for co-operation and help from all that were of her household.

She was the first teacher, for in the beginning there was neither priest nor pedagogue, and the school system of St. Louis began at the knees of the Creole mothers. She was the doctor. There was none other, and in time of sickness her limited knowledge of physic and her unlimited devotion as a nurse were gladly given within her house and out of it. Her hands were never idle, for when not engaged in showing others what to do she sewed and knitted warm clothing against the coming of winter; gave the personal touch to housekeeping and cleaning; after which, for relaxation, she retired to the kitchen, where with the help of Melisse, the cook, and her myrmidons, she concocted those marvels that have made Creole cooking the best cooking in the world to those who understand what good cooking is. She specialized in cordials and preserves, and some of the most treasured contents of the cellar were her blackberry cordial, cherry bounce, and gooseberry wine. As for pralines and gumbo soup, she discovered them and made them to perfection. No party was ever complete without them, and who will assert that they have been surpassed by any culinary achievement in history? Small wonder it is that under such teaching, the negro cooks of St. Louis became famous.

As for the men, *cés autres la,* they were a brave and resourceful lot, or they would not have been there. They were of the people who developed Canada from the North, and Louisiana from the

South; *coureurs de bois, voyageurs,* pioneers of France in the New World. Remote here from the strife that made a battle ground for generations of the eastern colonies, the lives of these men were given over to peaceful development of the land. After the manner of their race, when so permitted, they kept the peace with their neighbors, and save for the disturbance in *"L'année du Grand Coup,"* as the year of attack on the quiet village was called, no sound of strife was ever heard to disturb the quiet settlement by the river. They labored diligently in the making of their homes, in trapping and in trading with the natives for the furs that were their main source of wealth.

Habits and Manners

The dress of the pioneers, like their furniture, was at first restricted to what was stout and fit for their primitive surroundings. Simple and easy and often ill-fitting apparel of woolen or cotton material was worn according to the seasons. On Sundays and feast days some had a little silk finery laid by from the old days in Kaskaskia or New Orleans, but for the most part few were able, had they wanted, to overdress in a community engaged for six days of the week in wresting their very existence from the land. The men wore an outer garment with a hood, serving for overcoat and called a *capote.* It was commonly made from blanket material and can be found to this day among the Canadian woodsmen. Their shirts were of cotton, printed in gay patterns of stripes or flowers, breeches of cotton or of tow, with leather leggings. Some wore shoes, of a sort, but many preferred the Indian moccasin or, that superb combination of boot and moccasin, the *bottes sauvages.* In summer, a brightly colored kerchief bound around the head; in winter, a cap of coon skin; a particolored sash woven of hard worsted; leather belt, with sheath knife and tobacco pouch, completed their equipment. The women wore gowns of calico, for the most part, in the milder seasons, and of calimanco, a sort of mohair, in winter, with a kerchief around their shoulders, and *sabots* or moccasins for foot gear. It was only later, when luxuries began to be received from New Orleans, that the simple apparel of the pioneer gave way to the more costly and elaborate fashions of the cities. Within ten years after the founding we find record of the extensive importation of ornaments and luxuries, such as, silver buckles, stockings, both black and purple, silk in the piece, scarlet cloth, double-faced flannel for cloaks, lace edging, hats, silk handkerchiefs, snuff boxes, collar buttons, silk galloon, leather gloves, mirrors, lawns, muslins, and similar articles.

Despite the limitations of their wardrobes, the women in their freshly laundered dresses were ever, according to their wont, of appearance far neater than the men. These latter seem to have demanded occasions somewhat out of the ordinary to justify the effort of exchanging their comfortable foot gear for shoes and buckles; or of discarding tow and calico for their ceremonial vesture of fine cloth.

The final touch to their misery came with the substitution of powder and ribbons for the eel skin in which their hair was confined. This was as far as they went, and they did it seldom, until the beginning of that more splendid era, when the Spanish officers came and set an example of smartness that must needs be followed, if caste were worth saving. But long years were to follow the first settlement of St. Louis before it became possible to import heavier articles of furniture or the necessary appliances of agriculture. Not only did the first comers make their own chairs and tables, but they fashioned the very plows from the curved roots of trees.

Hauling was done in long narrow carts with harness of rawhide, that pulled out of shape in hot or wet weather. A sort of dray was also used, such as was often seen in the streets of the city a few years since. This vehicle was essentially a long narrow platform with heavy shafts at one end, mounted on a pair of huge wheels, the whole of stout construction and fit for hauling heavy loads. For lighter duty a *charette* was employed. This was a smaller cart mounted on two tireless wheels, quite similar to one employed, within the writer's recollection, in the remote villages of Quebec, save only that the modern innovation of tires had been added.

The prices of what was not produced by the colonists themselves were often high, on account of the cost of transportation. Coffee and sugar sold around two dollars the pound, and up to the time of the Louisiana Purchase tea was practically unknown. In the inventory of Charles Gratiot, gunpowder is listed at twenty *livres* the pound, or about four dollars. Some staples were inventoried at relatively low prices, among them, glass beads, tools, weapons, paints, glass, combs, etc.

SOCIAL CHARACTERISTICS

The jurisdiction of Spain was not onerous. The Spanish officials were respected for their fairness and loved for their good comradship. Their policy was constructive and their relations with the inhabitants the kindliest. Their passing offered no cause for rejoicing.

At the time with which we deal the settlement had reached a fair state of development and the lives of the people equalled in comfort and, to some measure, in luxury those of many of the older colonies. A resourceful citizen brought a piano from New Orleans. Its arrival was an event indeed and marked the commencement of a musical epoch.   Of painting there was very little.   It is true that traveling artists came this way, but their work was, for the most part, atrocious.   Yet, there were exceptions; witness the spirited likeness of Madame Chouteau, and of a few others of less note.   Later on, much later, came Carl Frederick Wimar, to whose splendid work is due the best record on canvas of characteristic scenes of the early West.   The portraits of De França, again later, have given us the likenesses of many of the earlier generations of St. Louisans.

Although the first piano was long upon its way, it must not be supposed that its notes were the first to gladden the hearts of the people.   Far from it, for when one dances there must be music, and is it conceivable that there could exist a village of good French Creoles where there was no dancing?   There were two violinists, Tardif and Chevreuil, or it might have been better, considering the times, to have called them fiddlers, who officiated early and late on these occasions.   History does not record their real names, but it has been handed down that they were easily among the most popular of the inhabitants. Afterwards there was better music and more able musicians, but that was in later years when the village had begun to put on the state and dignity of a city.

The general living conditions were, in many ways, like those of the French settlements on the lower St. Lawrence in our own times, and the beautiful story of Maria Chapdelaine, had its plot been laid in colonial St. Louis, well might have served to depict the manners and customs of our forefathers.

At first there was no church or resident priest and the spiritual needs of the people were served by neighboring missionaries.   It is needless to say that this condition did not long endure.

The first Mass in St. Louis was said in a tent. Our earliest record of a building for this purpose is of date 1770, when Father Gibault, then acting Vicar General of the Archdiocese of Quebec, blessed a wooden church which seems to have been the first of any kind erected. Père Valentin of the Capuchins was the first to administer to the "Parish of St. Louis and its dependencies."

In 1776 a larger church was built which served the town for many years. It was constructed of vertical timbers and measured thirty feet in width by a depth of sixty feet. The contract for building it was let to one Pierre Baron *dit* Lupien at a price of 1200 livres, to be paid in shaved deer skins. He died without completing it, and Jean Cambas undertook to do so, at a further cost of 1480 livres in similar currency. Later in the year, arrangements were made for the building of a parish house on the same land. The Catholic faith was that of all the inhabitants, and the parish priest was a personage of no small importance. He was the friend of each of his flock and his presence, as an honored guest, was taken as a matter of course at all functions, social, civic, and spiritual. It must be remembered that "To the French settlers, their religion was of the utmost importance . . . Their religion was not harsh and uncompromising, but sympathetic and indissolubly linked with their pleasure as well as their sorrows." Although the religion of the village was that of the church by law established for the colony, its administration was in no wise harsh or arbitrary. The spirit of intolerance did not range beyond the Mississippi river, and the black shadow of agnosticism had not darkened the simple and unquestioning belief of the inhabitants. The parish church often served for the adjustment of relations that are now commonly ratified in a lawyer's office, for contracts were there often entered into, orally, in the presence of the priest, after mass.

Inasmuch as the teachings of the Church did not proscribe innocent pleasure on Sunday, the inhabitants, who were very fond of dancing, did not refrain therefrom on that day. The women were especially reputed among travelers who have written of their voyages, for their gracious manner, their graceful dancing, and for their great beauty. As to this latter attribute, no historian is needed to record it, for the descendants of these same women exhibit a beauty to this day that is seldom equalled in America.

Sports, in the sense that we understand them, were not so well known in the infancy of the settlement. The lives of this people were, for the most part, spent out of doors, and the axe and the paddle, the rifle and the plough, used strenuously, and understandingly, gave sounder training to eye and limb than can ever be expected from their modern substitutes, the golf club and the tennis racket. Not that there were no out-door diversions. A favorite pastime, especially for the women and children, was excursions to the neighboring hills to gather berries; expeditions (not too lightly undertaken), to visit their acquaintances in the remote village of *Videpôche,* properly called Carondelet. All of the settlements were known by nicknames. St. Louis was called *Paincourt,* not for the lack of bread, but because flour had to be brought from a distance. Sometimes, these daring pleasure seekers ventured as far as distant Ste. Genevieve, but such an enterprise was not entered upon without grave preparation, including testamentary dispositions. Indeed, our forefathers showed no small concern as to the distribution of their belongings after their departure from this life, for it is said that the habit of making wills on slight provocation was an obsession with them.

And yet their lives were cheerful—very. They

took their work seriously, but they possessed the inestimable gift of quick reaction therefrom. Their worries did not follow them home, and when the day was done, the happy rites of hospitality, the relaxation of the dance, or, for the elders the sober study of the cards, at loo or bezique, bridged the gap between sundown and the hour, none too late, when they must needs take their rest.

The story of their doings has been told in many a sober history, but its incidents are of necessity barred for lack of space in the limits of this article. There are pictures that might be suggested, that are filled with color and the high lights of heroism. The story of Mme. Rigauche, the village school teacher, with rifle in hand, facing the Indians in the attack on the village; the narrative of the departure of the *bateaux,* filled with hardy *voyageurs* for the Indian country and the up-river trading posts, and of their homecoming; that of the merrymaking at the happy seasons of *Nöel* and the *Jour de l'an*—all of these are well worth recalling.

The memory of these *voyageurs,* the men and women who found their abiding place in the "village under the hill," is one to be happily treasured by their descendants and by all that dwell within the city that they founded. They were of France, the land that has given her best, here and elsewhere, in the cause of civilization.

Their leaders were of gentle birth,—gentlemen adventurers if you please, but they were as high minded as they were gentle. The controlling motive that led them into the untrodden wilderness of North America was *pro Deo et regi,* and even when they knew at the last that their king had forsaken them, they were true to his memory, while the Faith was served so long as the colony endured.

It has been asked whether the lives of the early settlers were happy, or their existence as Arcadian

as it has been depicted. Perhaps it was not. There
was sickness and suffering among them, and death
and the sorrow that follows, even as with ourselves.
But there are other thoughts that their story suggests. They were of one race, almost of one family,
with one Faith and one purpose, and while all so
remained they did well. They were hardy and intelligent and ever cheerful: the wilderness that they
found was one that abounded in all the riches with
which nature is vested. Why should they not have
been happy, or their existence Arcadian?

The old order changed; the *voyageur,* who first
ventured into the unexplored valley, who felled the
trees and built the houses that first were St. Louis,
is now but a gallant memory. Of him, as was written
of his brothers in Canada, we may say,

> " * * * his heart was young and his heart was light
> So long as he's leevin dere;
> I'm proud of de sam blood in my vein,
> So we'll fill her up till de bottle's drain
> And drink to de Voyageur."

JAMES CALLAWAY IN THE WAR OF 1812

Letters, Dairy, and Rosters[1]

By EDGAR B. WESLEY

The demands of the British commissioners during the negotiation of the Treaty of Ghent reveal the importance which England attached to the Mississippi river and the surrounding region. They insisted upon the creation of an Indian state, the free navigation of the Mississippi, and the principle of *uti possidetis*. They proposed an Indian country above the line of the Treaty of Greenville, and when that proposal was rejected,[2] they asked that the Indians be included in the peace treaty.[3] The navigation of the Mississippi, which had been conceded in the Treaty of 1783, presented a complicated problem, for the Louisiana Purchase and the declaration of war in 1812 altered the situation if they did not actually abrogate the original agreement.[4] Even though the matter was left unsettled, its discussion indicates the importance of the western region. The third proposal, that each nation retain what it then possessed, would have been of fateful consequence to the Mississippi country had it prevailed, for the Indians and British controlled the river as far south as the site

[1] The Missouri Historical Society received the Callaway Collection from the late Mr. Joseph Maher of St. Charles, Missouri. The letters and diary, here published, constitute the principal part, the rest being rosters, tax lists, and miscellaneous letters and notes.

[2] When the negotiations were temporarily broken off, the report reached the frontier that "The principal cause was the question relating to the Indians." Alfred Edward Bulger, "Last Days of the British at Prairie du Chien," in *Wis. Hist. Coll.*, XIII, 155-156.

[3] Henry Adams, *History of the United States*, IX, 18-19, 28; Frank A. Updyke, *The Diplomacy of the War of 1812*, 201, 208, 210, 216-217, 226. These writers give the facts and cite the sources.

[4] Adams, *op. cit.*, IX, 44-46; Updyke, *op. cit.*, 217, 300, 319-321.

of Fort Madison. The people along the Mississippi believed that the British planned the complete conquest of the river.[5]

The fortunate outcome of these questions has obscured the dangerous possibilities, and the minor scale of military operations has led to a minor consideration by historians.[6] The war in the East has received due emphasis, and the recent interest in William Henry Harrison has led to fairly detailed study of the war in the Ohio region,[7] but there was no man of comparable importance to unify the story or inspire a similar review of the events along the Mississippi. Everything which made the war important in the Old Northwest holds equally true of the Mississippi region with the tremendous addition of the river itself. If this viewpoint is reasonable, a new study of the War of 1812 which apportions due consideration to the Mississippi will have to be made.

The declaration of war in 1812 was something of a relief to the frontiersmen. They had suffered repeated outrages at the hands of the Indians and were hampered in their retaliation by the nominal peace. The war gave them unlimited opportunity to secure revenge and to proceed against the British whom they regarded as the source of most of the attacks. However, the British who took part in the war along the Mississippi were few, and in operation it was essentially an Indian war. It assumed no

[5] Christian Wilt Letters, Missouri Historical Society. This idea was strengthened by the Battle of New Orleans, for the news of peace had not reached St. Louis.

[6] William James's taunting remark, written in 1818, still indicates the historical status of 1927: "Neither the dislodgement of the Americans from Prairie du Chien, nor the affair between the Indians and the American armed barges, ascending the Mississipi [sic] . . . is noticed in any American history that we have seen." *Military Occurrences of the late War*, II, 190.

[7] Dorothy Burne Goebel, *William Henry Harrison;* Beverley D. Bond, Jr., "William Henry Harrison in the War of 1812," in *Miss. Val. Hist. Rev.*, XIII, 499-516.

great objective proportions, but the armies were by no means insignificant in view of the population,[8] and in view of their importance and the area which they covered.

The defense of the Mississippi region may be considered as twofold, protective and military.[9] The fear of Indian attacks led to the widespread erection and occupation of forts, a custom that was designated as "forting." Wherever several families could conveniently get together, they erected a blockhouse. In case the number of families to be accommodated was large, several cabins were erected in a rectangular arrangement, each with its projecting story and necessary loopholes. Palisades connected the outer sides of the buildings, and a considerable space was thus enclosed. Not every cabin which was called a fort deserved the designation, but several were important because of their size or location. Some forts existed before the war, but most of them were erected in 1812. The Missouri frontier, being the more exposed, took to "forting" first, but the Mississippi frontier was not far behind.

The northernmost post of a local nature was Fort Mason, near the site of Hannibal.[10] Southward, in what is now Pike county, were Fort Buffalo, two miles below the present Louisiana, and a post near the site of Clarksville. Wood's Fort, Stout's Fort, and Clark's Fort were in what is now Lincoln county. Fort Howard, named in honor of the governor, was an

---

[8] The population of the Territory of Louisiana in 1810 was 20,845; that of Illinois Territory, 12,282.

[9] A third defensive measure might be designated as diplomatic, for many efforts were made to secure the neutrality, if not the active assistance, of the Indians, and some of the Sac and Fox were temporarily detached from the British side. Some forty or fifty Shawnee and Delaware accompanied Dodge's expedition up the Missouri in 1814.

[10] Louis Houck, *History of Missouri*, III, 136-138. Houck locates most of the forts, but errs in some cases.

unusually large fort near the mouth of the Cuivre and the present village of Old Monroe. It accommodated between twenty and thirty families, and its erection required the labor of sixty men for two or three weeks. It was designed to supplant several family forts.[11] Rumors that the Indians of the upper Mississippi planned an attack led to the erection of a fort directly on the Mississippi in the summer of 1813. The site selected was eight miles above the mouth of the Cuivre and opposite a sandstone cliff on the Illinois side. The fort was smaller than Fort Howard, yet it was large enough to enclose several families. It was named Cap au Gris and was placed under the command of Capt. David Musick.[12] In the St. Charles District were Fort Howell on Howell's Prairie, southwest of St. Charles; Zumwalt's Fort, near O'Fallon; Castlio's Fort, near Howell's Prairie; Kountz's Fort, eight miles west of St. Charles; Fort Peruque, on the stream of that name; and Pond Fort, southeast of the site of Wentzville. In what is now Warren county were Kennedy's Fort, near the present Wright City; Callaway's Fort, near Charette; and Boone's Fort, the largest one in the section, near the Missouri. On Loutre Island were Talbot's Fort,[13] and Fort Clemson. In the Boon's Lick country were McLain's Fort, near the site of New Franklin; Fort Kinkead, about a mile above the site of Boonville on the north side of the river; Head's Fort, four miles above the present town of Rocheport, Boone county; the first Fort Cole, east of Boonville; the second Fort Cole, an unusually large one, near the present East Boonville; McMahon's Fort, five miles from the site of Glasgow, and Cooper's Fort, a large stockade flanked by log houses sufficient for twenty families, near the present

[11] John Shaw, "Narrative of . . .", in *Wis. Hist. Coll.* II, 205.
[12] *Ibid.*, II, 209. It was sometimes called Fort Independence.
[13] Houck, *History of Missouri*, III, 136.

Glasgow. There were other forts of a local nature, but these indicate the wide extent and great importance of this method of defense during the war.

In addition to these temporary family forts there were three regular government posts which were occupied by garrisons at the outbreak of the war: Fort Osage, on the Missouri, near the present town of Sibley, Jackson county; Fort Madison, in what is now southeastern Iowa; and Bellefontaine, on the south side of the Missouri, a few miles above its mouth. Small garrisons of regular troops occupied the forts and performed various duties relating to expeditions and protection.

The building of forts was equally popular in Illinois. By March, 1813, twenty-two forts had been erected in an irregular line from the mouth of the Missouri to the Kaskaskia river, sixty miles to the east. Scouts were sent between the posts daily, and spies scoured the country for miles beyond the occupied regions.[14] The principal forts, located by reference to present geographical terms, were: Journey's Fort, Aviston, Clinton county; one at Carlyle in the same county; Hill's Fort and Jones's Fort in Bond county; Chamber's Fort, near Lebanon; one at the mouth of the Illinois; one on Marcot Prairie on the west bank of the Illinois nineteen miles above its mouth; one opposite the mouth of the Missouri; one near Troy, Madison county; seven in White county; and Fort or Camp Russell, near Edwardsville, which was the most important post in Illinois during the war. The regular post at Fort Massac was also garrisoned, but it was too far from the frontier to be of great importance.[15]

[14] *Missouri Gazette*, March 20, 1813.

[15] Frank E. Stevens, "Illinois in the War of 1812," in Ill. State Hist. Soc., *Publications*, IX, 71-72. This article, covering pages 62-197, consists largely of letters, reports, and speeches made to and by the Indians.

The frontiersmen had learned from experience that the national government would not and perhaps could not protect them against Indians. Although the regular army had been increased from time to time because of rumors of war, it consisted of only 6,686 men in July, 1812; whereas the authorized strength was 35,603.[16] The garrisons in the west were reported as follows on June 6, 1812, just before the declaration of war: Forts Bellefontaine, 134; Osage, 63; Madison, 44; Massac, 36; Dearborn, 53; Vincennes, 117; Wayne, 85; and Mackinac, 89.[17] The war led to various rearrangements, and on August 23 it was estimated that only twenty regulars remained at Bellefontaine, and that about twenty occupied Fort Mason, which had not previously been a United States fort.[18]

To supplement the regular forces, the militia was called out from time to time, and companies of volunteers and rangers were authorized and raised. The law of January 2, 1812, empowered the president to accept the services of six companies of rangers for a period of one year, and the law of July 1 added an additional company; that of February 25, 1813, authorized ten additional companies, and the act of July 24 continued the laws for one year, and a final renewal for one year was passed on February 24, 1814.[19] Under these laws several companies of rangers were raised in Missouri and Illinois. On May 1, 1813, the nation was divided into nine military districts. The Eighth, consisting of Kentucky, Ohio, and the territories of Indiana, Michigan, Illinois, and

---

[16] Emory Upton, *The Military Policy of the United States*, 92.

[17] *American State Papers, Military Affairs*, I, 320.

[18] Christian Wilt Letters, Missouri Historical Society.

[19] U. S., *Statutes at Large*, II, 670, 774-775, 804; III, 39-40, 98.

A law of August 2, 1813, specified the organization of the company which was to contain altogether one hundred and nine men. *Ibid.*, II, 74.

Missouri, was placed under the command of General Harrison, with Illinois and Missouri as a sub-district under General Benjamin Howard.[20] This arrangement insured unity of control, but the vast extent of thinly populated country and the nature of Indian warfare rendered all measures unsatisfactory, and the constant changing of troops produced the results usually attending such military rotation.[21]

The war along the Mississippi began earlier and lasted later than in other sections, for, being largely an Indian war, it may be viewed as a continuation of the uprising started by Tecumseh in 1811,[22] and one affair of some importance, the attack on Cotes sans Dessein, occurred as late as April, 1815. The principal events of the war in the Mississippi sector were: the evacuation of Fort Osage, June, 1813,[23] Governor Edwards's expedition to Peoria, October, 1812;[24] the various attacks on Fort Madison and its evacuation, September 3, 1813;[25] General Howard's expedition to Peoria, September-October, 1813; the occupation of Prairie du Chien, June 2, 1814, and the building of Fort Shelby; the capture of Prairie du

[20] *American State Papers, Military Affairs*, I, 387, 432.

[21] Historians, as well as local chroniclers, have failed to distinguish between regulars, volunteers, rangers, and militia. In fact such differentiation is difficult, for no systematic study of the problem has been made. Upton's *Military Policy of the United States* is the nearest approach, but it attempts to cover an extended field, abounds in errors, and does not even mention the troops along the Mississippi in the War of 1812. This divided and opportunist policy is important, for, as Upton well shows, it resulted in the military debacle of the United States in the War of 1812.

[22] Forsyth Collection, Missouri Historical Society; Archibald Wilson Webster, Western Preliminaries of the War of 1812, Master's Thesis, Washington University.

[23] Letter Book C, 1812-1816, Indian Office, Washington.

[24] Edward's account is found in Ninian W. Edwards, *History of Illinois*, 69-72.

[25] *Niles' Weekly Register*, III, 142-143: "Ft. Madison," in *Annals of Iowa* (Third Series), III, 97-110; Frank E. Stevens, *Black Hawk War*, 38.

Chien by the British, July 19, 1814;[26] Lieut. John Campbell's expedition and the Battle of Rock River, July 22, 1814;[27] Gen. Henry Dodge's expedition against the Indians near Fort Osage, August-September, 1814;[28] Maj. Zachary Taylor's expedition to Rock river and the Battle of Credit Island, September 5, 1814, and the building of Fort Johnson in September and its evacuation and destruction in October, 1814. Besides these major events there were numerous attacks, massacres, skirmishes, and smaller expeditions.

James Callaway, the subject of this article, took part in Howard's expedition, the Battle of Credit Island, and the building and occupation of Fort Johnson; so a general statement of these events seems necessary. On July 16, 1813, the Indians attacked Fort Madison for the ninth or tenth time, and General Howard determined to repel their southward advance and rid the frontiers of their depredations by making a foray into the upper Illinois river country where the powerful Potawatomi lived. This tribe was able to put more than a thousand warriors into the field,[29] and they were thought to have committed outrages on the west side of the Mississippi as well as in Illinois. In August Capt. Nathan Boone, with sixteen or seventeen picked rangers, of whom Callaway was one, was sent to reconnoitre a route for the army. They were attacked by the Indians on August 15 and were scattered and driven across the Mississippi. Their experience proved the necessity for the expedition, and the Illinois militia and rangers, assisted by some Indiana and Kentucky companies, moved northwest from Camp Russell and

---

26 James, *op. cit.* 189-190, Appendix No. 39; *Niles' Weekly Register*, VI, 242; *Missouri Gazette*, May 7, July 2, 30, Aug. 6, 1814.

27 *Missouri Gazette*, July 30, Aug. 6, 1814.

28 *Ibid.*, Sept. 17, 24, 1814.

29 Forsyth Collection, Missouri Historical Society.

crossed the Illinois three miles above its mouth. They marched in detached groups in order to meet and repel stray bands of marauding Indians and thus relieve the frontier. The Missouri troops crossed the Mississippi at Fort Mason on September 17 and joined the Illinois forces, making a total of fourteen hundred. [30]   General Howard was in command, assisted by Col. Alexander McNair, and Majors William Christy and Nathan Boone for the Missouri regiment and Col. Benjamin Stephenson, and Majors W. B. Whiteside and John Murdoch for the Illinois regiment.[31] The army marched along the Mississippi to a point near the site of Quincy and then turned eastward toward the Peoria town where it arrived September 29.[32]

In the meantime Col. Robert Carter Nicholas with two hundred regulars ascended the Illinois in armed boats. They explored the region, began the erection of the fort at Peoria, and repelled an Indian attack before the arrival of Howard and the main body of troops. After Howard's arrival he sent out detachments to pursue the Indians, but the men found the villages deserted. After destroying what provisions were found, they returned to camp. Howard then sent Major Christy up the river in two armed boats. Christy ascended the river to within seventy-five miles of Chicago but found no Indians. Major Boone with one hundred men was sent in the direction of Rock river, and he also reported that the country was deserted.

The main body of troops labored at the building of Fort Clark, at Peoria, from the second to the fifteenth of October, bringing the timber from across the lake.

[30] *Missouri Gazette*, Sept. 18, Oct. 2, 1813; Houck, *History of Missouri*, III, 113.

[31] Stevens, "Illinois in the War of 1812," in Ill. State Hist. Soc., *Publications*, IX, 146-147.

[32] *Ibid.*, 149-150.

The weather was unusually cold, and the officers decided that nothing more could be done; so upon the completion of the fort the troops returned to Camp Russell where they were disbanded on October 22.[33]

In July, 1814, the capture of Prairie du Chien by the British and the defeat of Campbell's expedition threw the frontiers into a panic and emboldened the Indians to make sallies further down the river. The settlers gathered in forts, and General Howard drafted the militia and gathered the rangers for an expedition against the Sac and Fox of the Rock river region. Parts of these tribes were friendly to the Americans, and the efforts to spare the friendly ones afforded a cloak of protection for the hostile ones who had committed most of the outrages for which the Potawatomi and other tribes had received the blame.

A force of four hundred and thirty militia and rangers[34] under Maj. Zachary Taylor left Cap au Gris for Rock river[35] on August 22. They reached Rock river on September 4, and after the Battle of Credit Island on the fifth, the troops retreated to the rapids below the site of Fort Madison.[36]

Major Taylor sent Captains Callaway and Whiteside with one hundred men to erect Fort Johnson on the east side of the river near the site of Warsaw, Illinois. The fort was well situated on a high bluff

[33] Stevens, *op. cit.*, 151-153; Callaway to his wife, October 5, 1813, *infra; Missouri Gazette*, Nov. 6, 1813.

[34] *Missouri Gazette*, Sept. 3, 1814. Taylor's report says there were 334 effective men. *Ibid.*, Sept. 17, 1814. Callaway says 290.

[35] General Howard wished to mislead the Indians into believing that the objective was Prairie du Chien, hoping thus to secure their withdrawal and an open route to Rock river. Even Callaway thought Prairie du Chien was the objective.

[36] No details of the battle are given since Callaway's letters and diary cover that event. The longest account is Taylor's report published in *Missouri Gazette*, Sept. 17, 1814; *Niles' Weekly Register*, VII, 137-138; Stevens, *Black Hawk War*, 52-54.

opposite the mouth of the Des Moines. The garrison was soon short of supplies, and Taylor declared that he would. withdraw if they did not arrive by the last of September. He held out, however, until about October 22 when the fort was burned and the troops withdrew to Cap au Gris.

James Callaway, whose general activities in the War of 1812 have been indicated in the preceding pages, was the son of Flanders Callaway and Jemima Boone, daughter of Daniel Boone.[37] He was born about twelve miles from Lexington, Fayette county, Kentucky, on September 13, 1783. The Callaways moved to Missouri about 1801 and settled near Charette Village, the present Marthasville, Warren county. James engaged in the fur trade and went to Kentucky in 1804 with his cousins, Boone and William Hays, to dispose of some furs.[38]

Callaway married Nancy Howell on May 9, 1805. Nancy, daughter of Francis Howell, was born in Newbury county, South Carolina, January 27, 1788. The Howells moved to Upper Louisiana in 1795 and first settled in the St. Louis District, near the Missouri River; about three years later they moved to Howell's Prairie in the St. Charles District, several miles southwest of St. Charles.[39]

From his marriage in 1805 until the beginning of the war in 1812 Callaway engaged in various activities. His education was only ordinary, but he had good natural talents, and an affable personality won him considerable local popularity. He was frequently engaged in some activity of a public nature. For

[37] The sources for Callaway's life are a sketch written by his youngest brother-in-law, Lewis Howell, and the miscellaneous letters, bills, receipts, and notes found among his papers. Unless otherwise indicated these are the bases for statements about his life.

[38] Hazel Atterbury Spraker, *The Boone Family*, 180.

[39] Mary Iantha Castlio, *Some Missoui Pioneers*, 8-9.

some years he was a deputy sheriff and collected taxes in the St. Charles District, and in 1808 he was appointed cornet of a troop of cavalry in the militia.[40] In the same year he was paymaster for the Clark expedition which built Fort Osage (Clark), paying Nathan Boone for his services as guide to the troops. In 1810 he was appointed secretary's assistant for taking the census of the St. Charles District, and in 1812 was appointed to administer oaths. In 1814 he served as administrator for a small estate. He had some financial dealings with General Howard who gave him a note for $400 on August 21, 1814, while they were at Cap au Gris, and just before the departure of Taylor's army.[41] The activity, however, which he most enjoyed was that of military affairs. His exact record is somewhat obscure, but he seems to have been a captain of a militia company of cavalry as early as 1810. He took great pride in drilling his men, and, although an agreeable and considerate officer, he did not hesitate to see that fines were imposed upon delinquents.[42]

Callaway's domestic life was happy, and he succeeded financially. He bought fifty arpents of land on the northwestern part of Howell's Prairie from Louis Crow,[43] and built a house on a small stream to which he gave the name Crout Run. The Callaways had three children, Thomas Howell, born in 1806; William Boone, born in 1807, and Theresa Etaline, born in 1811.[44] In 1814 Callaway bought an

[40] Thomas Maitland Marshall, *The Life and Papers of Frederick Bates,* I, 331, 332; II, 25.

[41] The administrators of the Howard estate hesitated to pay the note, and it was not until after Callaway's death that the claim was finally paid.

[42] The militia laws of the territory were not severe, and attendance seems to have been lax. District of Louisiana, *Laws* . . ., I, 42-46, 150-162, 252-253.

[43] List of Territorial Taxes, 1815, St. Charles County.

[44] Costlio, *Some Missouri Pioneers,* 19-20.

adjoining tract of one hundred and fifty arpents from Crow and as early as 1808 he owned at least one slave, and at the time of his death he owned four, valued at more than a thousand dollars.

Callaway's general movements during the war can be traced from his letters and from miscellaneous notes among his papers. Early in 1812 he was captain of militia and saw duty as a spy and frontier guard. From April 29 to May 18 he was captain of a troop of mounted riflemen who patrolled the region northeast of St. Charles. He continued his military service on the Mississippi frontier, going as far north as Stout's Fort, near the site of Auburn, in what is now Lincoln county. Some time in the early summer he became lieutenant in the company of rangers of which his uncle, Daniel M. Boone, was captain. In July he was stationed at Camp Pleasant on the Cuivre,[45] and in September and October he accompanied Howard's expedition to Peoria. In November he was on the opposite frontier, constructing Fort Clemson on Loutre Island. He spent part of the winter of 1813-1814 at home, but the spring of 1814 found him again on duty along the Mississippi. On July 14 he was appointed captain of his company of rangers, succeeding Daniel M. Boone who resigned on June 21; during the summer and fall he served under Taylor in the Rock river expedition. After the evacuation of Fort Johnson he returned to the western frontier.

During the winter of 1814-1815 he was on duty at Fort Clemson. The Indian raids continued, and early in March a band of thirty or forty Sac and Fox stole some horses from the settlers near Loutre Island.

---

[45] While at Camp Pleasant Callaway received a letter from Benjamin Emmons, a member of the newly established legislative house, who reported the progress of their activities. The letter indicates Callaway's interest in politics, for it was written in response to his request.

Callaway took fifteen men and rode hastily up the west side of Loutre creek in pursuit of the Indians who had left a clear trail in the mud. About two o'clock they discovered the horses in the the care of some squaws who fled upon their approach. The Indians had returned to the settlements to commit further depredations or else had lingered behind to lay an ambush for their pursuers. Lieut. Jonathan Riggs suggested that the expedition return by a different route, but Callaway rejected the proposal, thinking that such precaution was unnecessary, since he supposed there were not more than a half dozen Indians in the neighborhood.[46] About sunset as they descended into a little ravine near the junction of Prairie Fork with Loutre creek, they were fired upon. Callaway and one man were behind the others, leading the horses, and when the firing was heard, the man suggested that they escape, but Callaway refused and rushed on to regain the head of his troop. In doing so he was wounded three times, and his horse was killed. Hiram Scott, seeing that his captain was wounded, tried to take him up behind, but the horse, frightened or wounded, would not move. The Indians were closing in on them, and Scott hastily made his escape to the rear, while Callaway ran for the creek, thrust his gun to the bottom, and dived into the water. A pursuing Indian came up and shot him in the back of the head as he swam. Four or five others were killed and two wounded.[47]

A few days afterwards when the water was lower

[46] Some accounts give their conversation in detail and indicate that Callaway was headstrong, and insulting in his reply to Riggs. Callaway's last letter to his wife indicates the strain under which he had labored during the preceding days and nights, and it is reasonable to suppose that this weariness caused him to be impatient of a circuitous return.

[47] The dead men were Hutchins, Gilmore, James McMullen, and James McDermott; wounded, James Gleason and John Atkinson.

Flanders Callaway and several men visited the scene and discovered the body lodged against a willow tree below where the battle occurred. Callaway's gun was found sticking in the mud from which the waters had partly receded. He was buried on the hillside and a slab bearing the inscription "Captain James Callaway, March 7, 1815," was placed on his grave.[48]

Nancy Callaway was attending school[49] when she received word of the death of her husband. She left without a word and stoically walked home, but fainted as she entered the house. Her efforts to keep the farm in good condition and to care for the children while her husband guarded the frontier is an affecting testimony of her qualities. In 1818 she received a pension of twenty dollars a month, dating from her husband's death. She lived to the age of seventy-six, dying in 1864.[50]

Callaway was about six feet in height, rather slender, of dark but ruddy complexion, and was usually

[48] The exact details of this battle and of Callaway's death constitute a problem, for the numerous accounts differ on so many points. All accounts agree that the battle occurred on the same day the men started. If that is correct, it is hard to reconcile Callaway's last letter with the date universally given, the seventh of March. It is possible that all have taken it from the gravestone which could be in error. *Missouri Gazette*, March 11, 25, and April 1, 1815; Bryan and Rose, *Pioneer Families of Missouri*, 95-101; Houck, *History of Missouri*, III, 124-125; *S. H. Long's Expedition*, in *Early Western Travels* (Reuben Gold Thwaites, ed.), XIV, 133; Rufus Babcock, *Memoir of John Mason Peck*, 139; *History of St. Charles, Montgomery, and Warren Counties, Missouri*, 156-159; Samuel Gibson and Nathan Boone's accounts to Draper. (copied by Mr. Ovid Bell of Fulton, Missouri, whose kindness is cordially acknowledged) There are other accounts, but these probably contain about all the versions of the affair.

[49] One of the touching aspects of the Callaway correspondence is the fact that Nancy could not write. (Letter of May 9, 1814, *infra.*) She later learned to write a tolerable script. One letter which she certainly wrote, being of a legal nature, is in the Callaway Collection.

[50] In 1818 Mrs. Callaway married John Harrison Costlio by whom she had several children.

NANCY CALLAWAY CASTLIO
(Through courtesy of Miss Oleta Bigelow)

accounted a rather handsome man. His courage was unquestioned and his long and constant service endeared him to frontiersmen. He had a cheerful, kind, and affectionate nature which caused him to be an indulgent father and a kind master. His numerous activities gave him a wide acquaintance, and his qualities rendered him popular with all classes. Such men as Callaway were the ones who helped to establish that traditional respect for frontiersmen which has become a part of the American heritage.

LETTERS

Mouth Dardenne[51]
5th May 1813

Dear wife

I fondly imbrace this oppertunity of Informing you that I am well and your Brothers[52] also Larking[53] is Some what unwell but not Dangerously our Rout is from The portage De Soux[54] on one Day and Back to portage Desoux the Next about Sixteen Miles we Draw provision a plenty and corn I Calculated when I Left you to have returned to you before the twenty Days is out but I find that this fronteer above Mentioned is too Dangerous to be Left unguarded and as it is Consigned to the Care of the Company under my Command And it so small that I Do not think it

[51] The Dardenne flows northeast through St. Charles county and empties into the Mississippi about six miles above the mouth of the Illinois. Callaway's patrol thus covered a vital area.

[52] Her brothers, then in service under Callaway, were John, Thomas, Francis, and Benjamin Howell.

[53] Larkin S. Callaway was a younger brother of James. He was born in Kentucky in 1794, and married Susannah L. Howell, Nancy's younger sister, December 22, 1815. It is interesting to note that Thomas Howell married Susannah Callaway, making three alliances between the two families.

[54] Portage des Sioux was located on the west bank of the Mississippi about five miles below the mouth of the Illinois.

possible for me to Leave it at all I shall write you again Next week No Indians sign No Neus kys my Daughter for me and shake hands with the Boys give my Complimentes to Susannah and the rest of the family while I Remain your Lovin Husband untill Death

James Callaway

Mrs Nancy Callaway

Portage Desoux
9th May 1813

Dear wife

I am in perfect helth at present and your brothers also Larking is also got well   I am about to inform you with Respect to Indians news fully I belive as any person as I had it from General Howard[55] Himself and was this day in council with a party of sauxks and foxes and Peyankeeshaws Thay gave all information with respect to Dixon[56] and his Indians that they knew of they State the Last accounte from perara de Sha[57] was that Dixon had ben through all the nations on the Illenoies Mississippi and Rock River and Indians all agreed to come with him to

[55] Benjamin Howard was appointed governor of Louisiana Territory (Missouri) September 19, 1810, but his delay in taking charge and his absences often left affairs in the hands of Frederick Bates, Secretary and at various times Acting Governor. Howard was appointed a brigadier general on March 12, 1813, and William Clark became governor, July 1, 1813. Howard died at St. Louis, September 18, 1814.

[56] Robert Dickson was a British fur trader who operated from Prairie du Chien. He was very active and successful in enlisting the Indians on the side of the British. For a discussion see Ernest Alexander Cruikshank, "Robert Dickson, the Indian Trader," in *Wis. Hist. Coll.*, XII, 133-153.

[57] Prairie du Chien was a fur and trading post on the east bank of the Mississippi near the mouth of the Wisconsin in what is now southwestern Wisconsin. For a description of the place in 1811 see a letter of Nicholas Boilvin to the Secretary of War, in E. B. Washburne, ed., *The Edwards Papers*, 59-67; also printed in *Wis. Hist. Coll.*, XI, 247-253.

fight against St. Louis that dixon gave them Large presents such as Powder ball paint wompum &c &c they was to meet him at perara De sha aprel Last and when they asked Dixon where the British Was that was to bring the cannon and help them fight he Told them Their was an number of Traitors below at portage St Charles and St Louis That would assist them the Indians made answer that as thir was no British and he had made the failure they would Return home to their Villags and make their Corn and hunt for Meat for their famalies Dixon then told them that they must give up the presents they Had Recived of him they told him no that they had performed And was willing to perform provided he would fulfill his proposoition but as the faillure was entirely on his part that thay would keep His presents & go home too and did goo Since that Time a Mr forSythe[58] has come down the Illenoies river and stats that dixon is to be down the tenth of this Month to the Mouth of the Illenoies river where they are to Rendevux with a large numbe of Indians But for-siythe Is not Calld a man of Truth tharefore no Confidence Can Be placed on his Tale we are verry well prepared for their reception at this place as their is Capt Owens has a Company of artillery in A Gun boat and 60 men Capt Smith[59] has a gun boat and 60 men Capt Desha[60] has a good block house on the river and 100 men Regulars several six pounders and an

---

[58] Thomas Forsyth was an Indian trader and agent. He was born at Detroit, December 5, 1771, and died near St. Louis, October 23, 1833. During the War of 1812 he was stationed at Peoria where he acted as a secret agent for the United States. A collection of his papers belongs to the Missouri Historical Society.

[59] William Smith was captain of a volunteer company raised in 1812, and he had charge of other companies at later dates.

[60] Robert Desha of Tennessee became a captain in the regular army, March 12, 1812, and was breveted major for gallant conduct at the attempted recapture of Mackinac. He was a representative in Congress from Tennessee from 1827-1831.

Isleand in the middle of the River[61] well fortified that you may see the river for too mil[62]

Stouts fort[63] 11th June 1813

Dear wife

I have for a few Days Past been very unwell at the Present I am weak but mending verry fast. I had Started home a few Days ago but met Jesse Vanbibber[64] and some orders that obliged me to Return to my Encampment not withstanding my sickness I Expect I Shall be Down on saturday Next in order to go to Court I shall only have time to Stay a few Days we have no news no Indian sign Discovered on this frontier I wis[h] to see you verry much and also my Children[65] No more at present My Compliments to all enquireing frends

Your husband

Mrs. Nancy Callaway

61 This island, just below Portage des Sioux, was fortified in April, 1813, in accordance with General Howard's suggestion. Col. Daniel Bissell directed that the fort should have walls four and a half or five feet thick and seven feet high with a palisade to protect the sides. The post was occupied on May 10, 1813, by Capt. Charles Lucas, who named it Fort Lookout.

62 This letter is unsigned. It was written on the back of the preceding one.

63 Stout's Fort was a small stockaded post near the site of Auburn, Lincoln county.

64 Jesse Van Bibber was the second son of Peter Van Bibber, who came from Virginia to Missouri about 1803.

65 Their children and their ages at this time were, Thomas Howell, seven, William Boone, five, and Theresa Etaline, three.

Camp Near St Charles 15th June 1813

Dear wife

I am in Good Health and sincerely hope that these Lines may find you and my Dear Children in a good State of health I have nothing particular to write you at present we know not when we shall be removed from this place nor where we shall be marched to we have accounts Quite favourable from general Harrison we hear that he has Drove the British and Indians from his Quarter[66] and a number of the Indians wish to make peace their was a 60 or 70 went Down the Mississippi the other Day to St Louis to make peace for some of the rock river nations[67] I wish you to send by Oliver some buisquit butter cheese a bottle Shugar and some cloathes

I remain Dear wife your

Loving husband till Death

J. CALLAWAY

Mrs. Nancy Callaway
    Howells Station
Attention
F. Howell

Cappo Gray Sept 14th 1813

Dear wife

I am at this time in Perfect Health as also Brother Larking and your Brothers we have a full supply of Provisions our horses fet and able to perform the trip, I do not know where We are to go as yet and I believe no person will know untill we return I am now a Crossing the Mississippi in order to pilot the Troops that have came on from the Illinoies Terri-

---

[66] Harrison won a notable victory by repulsing Proctor's attack on Ft. Meigs during the first few days of May, 1813.

[67] The Sac and Fox who lived in the Rock river section were divided, but most of them took the side of the British.

tory to the place where we crossed the Mississippi
when the Indian routed us,[68] I expect we shall all
go to the Peori towns and Return from that Place
perhaps we may go to Rock River but I think not,
as our force is some what smaller than we calculated
it would be.[69] I think we shall be about fifteen Hundred strong as this is the Last time untill I Return
that I shall have an opportunity of writing to you I
wish you not to be uneasy about me make yourself
easey and as Comfortable as possible and as sure as
their is an opportunity of writing I shall send you a
Letter Rember me to my Dear Children and should I
never Return be Carefull in giving them good Learning if in your Power and teach them humanity and
genteellity I am in hopes of Returning again in the
Course of a month at which time I shall procure a
furlugh to be with you a few days and at the expira-
tion of my term of service I shall Quit the woods I
am Determined on it   Those Lines I write in good
Health and High sperits in hopes it will meet you
together with my Dear Children in the same way.
While I Remain untill Death Your Loving and ever
affectionate Husband

JA[s] CALLAWAY

N.B. some money in the hands of Deacon Cottle
for me

Mrs. Nancy Callaway
        Dardenne
             St Charles County
Attention Mr [John E] Allen

[68] In August General Howard had sent Capt. Nathan Boone with
Callaway and fifteen or sixteen rangers to reconnoitre the region
over which the army expected to march. They were attacked by
forty or fifty Indians and had to retreat across the Mississippi, without any loss, however, except the wounding of two men.

[69] Callaway's conjecture turned out to be correct, for the main
army did not try to go to the Rock river section.

October 5th 1813
Peorias Camp No 16 on the
east side of the Illinoies river

Dear wife I am at Present in good Health and Likewise the boys in my mess we have met with no Indians as yet we are prepareing timber for the fort and as soon as the fort is Completed I expect we Shall return home the army has been about twenty miles above this Place found Some Indian Plunder but no Indians and but Little sign it is generally beleived that all the mischief that has been done in the Course of the Sumer Past was Done by the Sacks as we have seen but Little sign since we left the missippi; our horses is verry much reduced; their has nothing material happened only one man killed by his own mess mate that belonged to Capt. Biggers Company.[70] So no more at present but remain

Your loving husband till Death

JA[S] CALLAWAY

Mrs Nancy Callaway
   St Charles County
      C/o Mackay Wherry Esqr.
      St Charles

Luter Isleand[71]
November the 24th 1813

Dear wife I have had my health since at this place but very Little untill at this time I have a tolerable

[70] Probably James Bigger, captain of a company of Indiana volunteers who took part in this expedition.

[71] Loutre Island is in the Missouri river, near the north bank, and is divided by the Warren-Montgomery county line. It is not a true island, being connected with the mainland during dry seasons. It was then about twelve miles long, very fertile and heavily wooded. It was settled probably as early as 1798, certainly by 1807, and became a flourishing settlement before the mainland was ever occupied. There were several forts near the island and at least two or three on it. The fort which Callaway erected was named Clemson in honor of Capt. Eli B. Clemson.

share, considerading the weather and the bad Camps; we have just got in our house Last knight before the snow fell it is not as yet verry Comfortable but we are at work as fast as possible the fort is as far forward as Could be expected I think the men will all get in their Quarters against Sunday knight the boys is well I Shall be Down between the first & tenth of next month Crow is to assist in getting in my Corn if the weather will admit of it. I have no news at all write to me by the first opportunity and remember me to the Children whilst I Remain your Husband

JA^S CALLAWAY

Nancy Callaway

Fort Clemson 19th March 1814

Dear and Loving Wife

With infinite satisfaction I Take up my Pen to inform you that I am hearty and well at this time and Likewise your Brothers, and feel gratified when I hope that these Lines will find you and my Dear Children well—I have no news to write you at this time, but if any should come to my years bilieve me that I shall take the earliest opportunity to apprise you of it, it will no Doubt be a great satisfaction to hear that I have Bought one hundred and fifty arpens of Land adjoining our Tract, of Lewis Crow and Paid him in full for it—one hundred and eighty Dollars and Paid two Hundred and twenty five Dollars to My father and the ballance of what Money I Collected I Paid My Debts and have a small sum Left to Devide with you and the rest of my friends—I am well a ware My Dear wife that I Put more on your shoulder than you are well able to bear but as it will be of great Importance to us both and a general advantage to the family, and as I know you are willing to bear a great burden to Promote Our welfare I wish If it is in your Power to Hire some Person to

Trim my apple Trees perhaps you could get Mr Stone[72] and if not him you Could get Brother Larking to do it as he Told me he should spend the greater part of his time with you I do not Know when I shall be able to Come Down I fear not untill my Time is out—as the officers all have been Confined here so Long that they are about to get furloughs and they only are to go one at a time and my Tour will Come Last that I expect I shall not Come Down untill my Time is out or at Least untill the first of May—I hope My Dear if you should meet with an opportunity that you will send the Children to school as it is and allways was my wish to send them to school.

so no more at Present But Remains Dear wife your Loving Husband untill Death.

JA^S CALLAWAY

Mrs Nancy Callaway

Block house on the Missippi
Near portage Desioux 1st May 1814

Dear wife

with heart felt Pleasure I take up my Pen to inform you that I am in good health and in hopes that you and my Little Children are well you have no Doubt heard of the Murder that has been Done near woods fort,[73] I Deplore your Lonesome situation in times of Difficulty but I do not think that you are in the Least Danger for you are surrounded on every side by famalies, and the Indians have never yet Dared to Commit murder in the settlements at any other Place than on the frontier, we have no news about the rangers whether they will be raised or not neither

---

[72] John B. Stone was cornet of one of Callaway's companies and helped him at various times with his work.

[73] The *Missouri Gazette* of May 7, 1814, says: "Last week a man of the name of M'Coy was shot and cut to pieces in the neighborhood of Wood's family fort, a few miles from St. Charles."

Do I Know when the boats will start from St Louis[74] I have heard that they are to start at Different time give my Compliments to Mr. Oden and to my Dear Children and accept the kind wishes for your welfare hapiness and good health from Dear wife your Loving and affectionate

JA^S CALLAWAY

N.B. I do not expect to come home untill my Time is out   J. C

Nancy Callaway
   Crout Run
      Mr Hutchens

Block house on the Mississippi[75]
Near Portage De sioux 9th May 1814

Dear wife

I am enjoying Perfect Health at This time and in hopes that these Lines will find you and the Children in good health I was in hopes that I should of re-

---

[74] This refers to Governor Clark's plans for the occupation of Prairie du Chien. The expedition, consisting of fifty or sixty regulars and about one hundred and forty volunteers, left St. Louis on May 1, and occupied the post and erected Ft. Shelby. Some of the troops returned to St. Louis on June 26, their period of enlistment having expired. *Missouri Gazette*, May 7, July 2, 1814.

[75] The receipt which was given to Callaway when he left the blockhouse is given in full since it indicates the equipment of a frontier post.

Reeceved of Lut. James Callaway all the Publick Property belonging to and about the Block house on the Mississippi Near portage Dessoux (viz.) two six pounders, mounted, two aminiiton Boxes— twenty one fixed Cartridgees—twenty three Blank Catriage: six canister of Balls—. fifty nine Six pound Balls three priming howitzers ten Brack howitzers two Shovels two sponges one pair of wipers three priming wires—four slicks port line two Drag Ropes fore lint stacks one yoke oxen. one cart one Cross Cut saw one pearouge one mare one bote and sixteen oars twenty two half pound Balls—

Arter [Arthur] Morgan
Secon leut us R

ceived a Letter from you by your brother but found
you had neglected me however I excuse you because
you Cannot write yourself and it is Difficult to get
any Person to write for you the other Day their was
a raft found near this Place supposed to be Indians
but we have found out that it was three Negroes
made it, so that we have no Indian News amongst us,
I Do not expect to Come home untill my time of
service expires it is now verry short and we have no
Orders for Raising another Company as yet I should
be verry glad to Come home one time more bifore we
are Discharged but as things are aranged it is out
of my Power therefore I must Content myself to stay
and Pass the Time as well as Possible Tell the boys
if they go to School and Learn well that I Will give
them a handsome Present when I am Done Ranging.
My Compliments to Mr Dozier and all enquiring
friends not forgetting my Dear Etteline and except
for your self the well wishes of Dear wife your ever
affectionat and Loving Husband

JA^S CALLAWAY

Mrs Nancy Callaway
   Crout run
      Mr. Ham

Stouts fort 5th June 1814

Dear Wife

I am at this time well, fortunately so for me, as
their is a Number of the men sick at this time I keep
Spies out constant they have made no Discoveries of
Indian Sign as yet it appears to be still Times on
the frontier at this time and I account for it in this
way all the Indians that Intends war is a watching
the movements of the armed boats under the command of Governor Clark but I am Determined not
to be Lulled to Sleep under those Impressions, I
shall be on the alert and keep out Spies and recon-
nitering parties in all Directions I should be verry

sorry if I should put you to trouble, in those times no person knows what to do for the Best, but every Person have a right to thir own opinion, and it is my Opinion that you move all our household furniture Home without the Least fear Now my Dear wife if you Should be of the Same oppinion have them brought home and then Should anything turn up so that they Should be Lost thir can be no reflections cast—Do not think that I am jealous of reflections being thrown on me, neather would I wish you to think that I am willing to Cast any on you—

I should be extremely glad to get a few Lines from you for it affords me a great satisfaction to hear from you and my Children, Tell them that nothing they Can Do will please me so much as to go to School and Learn to read and write, that as soon as they Can Spell well I shall give them each a Copy Book and Let them Learn to write; My Compliments to Mr Oden and all enquiring friends and accept for yourself the well Wishes of Dear wife your Loving and ever affectionate

JA^S CALLAWAY

Mrs Nancy Callaway
    Crout Run

Camp Stouts fort 15th June 1814

Dear wife

I Received your Letter of the 11th of this Inst. informing me that you ware all well Except my Daughter and I am in hopes that she will soon recover from her sickness as she only has the Measles Let her Drink warm Coffee Tea or some other warm Drink knight and morning and she will soon recover —You have no doubt heard that two of the citizens of Lower Quiver by the name of Ewings and a stranger from the State of Ohio, they ware at the Mill on sandy about 10 mile from Lower Quiver and about six from Cappo grais they were in the act of filing a saw and both Shot down[76] together they Lay untill they ware nearly eat up before they were found I have no other news at present

I remain in health your

Loving husband

JAS. CALLAWAY

Mrs Nancy Callaway
   Crout run
   per Express

Stouts fort twenty seventh of
June one thousand eight
Hundred and fourteen

Dear wife

I am in Perfect Health at Present in hopes that these Lines will find you in better health than when I left you, I know your situation is Lonesome and Disagreeable even when you are well, and it must be more so when you are sick, if you are not better I will steal time enough after muster to come and see you, and perhaps I may anyhow, your Brother Benjamin is sick but not Dangerous and your Brother francis started yesterday to the Sharrett with my father who has been in Camp to sell some powder, my father tells me he will let me have old Bill to Do the work, I wished to get a hand of Tolbert to Do, and I espect I shall buy Cach from Zumwalt if he will sell him[77] fifty five of my men has started for a Trip for fifteen Days and fifteen men and one Sar-

[76] No other account of these murders has been found. It is certain that the murdered men were not John, Patrick, or William Ewing, for John paid taxes in 1816: Patrick was married, December 28, 1815: and William was appointed an ensign on October 1, 1814. The account is too realistic to admit of doubt, but there might be some mistake of names.

[77] There is no evidence that he ever bought Cach, but on Dec. 22, 1814, he bought Martin, a nineteen year old boy, from his cousin William Hays for five hundred dollars.

gent has started from this Place under the command
of Lieutenant Riggs ordered with forty Days Provision to meet at Cappo grey on the first Day of
Next month in order to go to Perara De Sha[78] I have
no other news at this time I have sent the horse home
that I rode out here and want my horse from your
fathers that John Callaway Brought from St Charles

your Loving Husband untill Death

JA^S CALLAWAY

Mrs Nancy Callaway
    St Charles County
        Crout Run
Attention Col° D. M. Boone

Isleand Camp opposite Cappo Grais 9th August 1814

Dear father and Mother

I Take advantage of a few Leisure moments to
inform you that I am well at Present and I hope
when this Reaches you that you as well as the Rest
of the family will be enjoying good Health   You
will no Doubt Hear before this Reaches you of the
surrender of the Troops at perara Deshain[79]   I have
no orders at this time more than to lay here untill

[78] Lieut. John Campbell's expedition, consisting of forty-two regulars and sixty-six rangers, left St. Louis in July to strengthen the
garrison at Prairie du Chien. The troops occupied three boats and
the sutler and contractor furnished three additional ones. Prairie
du Chien was captured on the nineteenth, and on the twenty-second
the relief expedition was badly defeated at Rock river. *Missouri
Gazette*, July 30, Aug. 6, 1814.

[79] A large band of British and Indians attacked the newly erected
Ft. Shelby and the gun boat *Governor Clark* at one thirty on July
17. The boat was soon forced down the river, but the fort held out
until the evening of the nineteenth, and then surrendered because
the garrison had been weakened by the withdrawal of the men whose
terms had expired, because there was no doctor to dress the
wounded and because ammunition, water, and supplies were "almost
expended." Seven men were wounded on the *Governor Clark* and
five in the fort. *Missouri Gazette*, May 7, July 2, 30, Aug. 6, 1814.

further orders, my men are generally Healthy and in High Sperits I expect that I shall go on to the Perara as I understand that their is Large Drafts a making amongst the malitia

I feel in great Sperits myself, I have a verry good running Boat and well fortified—I think we are at the Defiance of the Indians unavoidable accidents expected I understand that an expedition is on foot against michilimakinak if they should be successful[80] we shall have easy times to what is generally expected at this time and at all events the attention of the Indians will be Drawn towards that place as it is a post of greater Importance than Perara Deshain it is the opinion of the officers from perari De Shain that the Indians will not be verry Troublesome Down this way only in scouting parties as the great boddy of warriors will be Drawn of to the north and against they return it will be too Late to Come Down, and besides they must have time to hunt provisions for their families to Live on in the winter season

Dear parents I mentioned in the foregoing part of my Letter that I was in high sperits you will understand that this sperit flows only when I think of the Voyage I have undertaken, and believing that a man embarking in his Country Cause is not only honourable but his Duty, and especially when it is invaded by a Cruel and savage foe. Should I Fall the Cause then will be an honourable one and I Trust no man may have it in his power to add a cowardly one, and, I want no person to greive for me, but when I Consider that I am connected to a woman worthy of every blessing and calculated to render me entirely happy; to leave her together with my Darling Infants unprotected in a savage world my high millitary sperits falls below par, and I am almost Readdy to resign my Commission, but a moment Reflection with Respect to the

---

[80] The expedition was a failure.

situation of my Country together with this consideration that their is a number of men that has Joined the service that would not if any other person Commanded makes me Quit such Thoughts—Their is no man that Longs for a Private Life than I do, but I am at a great distance from it at present should you have an opportunity to call and Consolate my wife in her forlorn situation it would be   Truly gratifying to me, with sincere wishes for your health welfare and hapiness I Remain sincerely your Dutiful son

JA^S CALLAWAY

Mr Flanders and Jamimah Callaway
   St Charles County
      Sharette Village

August the 15th 1814 Camp Near Cappo Grais

Dear wife

I Received your favour of the 13th Inst which gave me great satisfaction to hear that you ware all well. I am sorry that you are reduced to the Necessaty of moving from home, but I am greatly in hopes that your mind will be more at rest than if you ware at home so Lonesome as you must be, and I could almost wish you to let the boys go to School if your Brothers Do but you must be guided by your good judgement as you are their and know more and better how to manage affairs than I Can advise you at this distance. If you act your own judgement you will Please me and most Certainly you will Please yourself or at Least you can have no Person to Blame if you could get any Person to get out my wheat it would be a help to you and if you was to give one third for getting the ballance out it would be better than to Loose the whole

I still hold good sperites and Enjoy Perfect Health no news nor no orders since I wrote you before no Indian sign on this frontier   Remember

me to my Dear Children your Mother and all
enquireing friends I Remain Dear Wife your
Loving Husband Hoping for your Health I am

JA^S CALLAWAY

Miss Nancy Callaway
      Howells Fort
Mr Bowen.

Lower Rapids on the Mississippi[81] 6th Sept 1814

Dear wife   For the first time since I Left Cappo
grais I Rejoice at an opportunity of writing to you
to Let you know that I am well at present although
it has not been so Long for in three Days after I
Left Cappo grais I was taken with the fever and
ague and it Continued untill three Days ago it Left
me and I Recover my strength verry fast we are
on our return from Rock River and at this Place
we have to build a fort and as soon as that is Completed I shall be Down—

I must now inform you that we had a severe battle
with the Indians and british at Rock River[82] which
Lasted about six hours and here I will give you the
particulars as they occur to my mind we arived at
Rock river on the evening of the 4th of Sept and
the first objects that presented themselves to our
view was the Plains Covered with horses in a miles
Travel we Discovered a Canoe Loaded with Savages
we hoisted a white flag but they run into the woods
we went on a Little farther and their was a few
savages say two Hundred that apaerd to our view
but they ware on each shore and we on an Isleand

---

[81] This letter was written from the post which was soon afterwards named Ft. Johnson. It was on the site of the present town
of Warsaw, Illinois, and opposite the mouth of the Des Moines, on
a bank ninety feet above the river.

[82] This battle occurred at Credit Island, on the west side of the
Mississippi, in what is now a part of Davenport, Iowa.

we stopt and cooked our suppers still shewed our
white flag but of no use we ware obliged to stay at
the shore all knight for the wind blew a Hurricane;
about three Hours before Day the Indians commenced a fire on our Centinels and wounded two of
them at Day Light we were ordered to go and scour
the Isleand which we succeeded in doing in this I
had one man wounded and Capt whitesides[83] had one
we killed one Indian, we was then ordered to our
boats the wind blew still verry hard and prevented
us from manoevering but Capt Rector[84] was ordered
Down to the Lower end of the Isleand to prevent the
savages from crossing to the Isleand that we occupied—all was well then as we thought but in this
we ware Deceived for in the night the Brittish had
thrown up a battery on the opposite side of the
River at the Distance of about six Hundred yards
and just as the boat Droped Down to the Lower
end of the Isleand they opened a fire on our boats
from one six one four and one three Pounders the
first shots flew over us for fifteen or twenty five
but they found out their mistake and began to
Lower thir peices and they stuck them in to our boats,
masts, sails stering oars and at Last was base
enough to knock the Splinters into the men's faces
we Returned the fire from our swivels and small
arms but found we could not hurt them owing to
the Distance We Droped Down about three miles
and they fired at us all the Time with small armes
and instead of the Horses we saw the evening before
on the plains it was lined with savages armed and
fireing at us we kept up the fire at them with our
swiivels small arms &c we had about two hundred
or more after we Dropt Down their was a Council
of war held by the officers and it was thought best

---

[83] Samuel Whiteside of the Illinois rangers.
[84] Stephen Rector of the Illnois rangers.

to give up the persuit as we ware not able to erect a bettery on shore so that we Could play our six pounder on the place we wanted it and if we built our battery below we could not ingure them so we thought best to Come off and so we Did we had ten men wounded one of them we buried this morning and I think one or two others will Die shortly; only one man in my company is slightly wounded Silvenus Cottle. I expect to be at home against the twentyeth or twenty fifth give my Compliments to all enquireing friends and except for yourself the well wishes of your

JAS. CALLAWAY

N B Your Brothers have the fever and ague and is verry thin in the Jaws but I'll fetch them home with me

J C

Mrs Nancy Callaway
Howells Station

Fort Johnson, East side Mississippi Foot of
the Lower Rapids
25th Sept 1814

Dear wife

You will no Doubt (from my Last Letter to you) be a Looking for me in Person instead of this Small Peace of Paper which I send to you as a token of Love and friendship—a man in the service situated as I am is tossed and Carried about Like a Ship on the sea without a Rudder or a man to Steer her he may make calculations how and when he will go, but if a storm rises he is Drove a Contrary Course Such is the Case with me at Present, but it shall not always be so, I am ordered to Remain at this Place with fifty of my own men and fifty of Capt whitesides company how long I know not, but I expect to be Relieved in twenty or twenty five Days

we have only had one attact made on us since we
were at this Place and in that one only one man
wounded we have our fort finished and it is verry
Strong and their will be an addition to the Rangers
about forty five Regular Troops two six and one
three pounders and two swivels we have not more
than ten Days of provisions for the Troops at this
place and I am assured by Majr Taylor that if Provisions does not Reach this place against the Last
of this month that the post will be Evacuated and
all the men Come Down[85] I have no news to write
you but I should be extremely glad if you Could Con
vey a Letter to me as I am extremely anxious to hear
from you and the Children for they are at all Leasure
Hours on my mind, and my Leisure Hours are but
few since at this place for I have been either officer
of the Day or officer of the fatigue party every Day
since I Came here after this my Duty will Not be
Hard unless the Indians commence an attack on us,
when I Return if I find all peaceble Times I mean to
stay four or five weeks at Home and Have my
affairs on the farm fixed in some small Degree Comfortable for the winter   Should I not hear from you
I Shall expect that you have had no opportunity of
writing to me as I Do not expect you would Let one
Slip by you   I have riquested Mr. Becknell[86] to go
to Genl Howard and Know of him how Long I am to
Stay at this place and if I am to Stay here he will
Call and see you and you will Send me Some winter
cloathes, sugar, Cheese, butter   Give my Compliments to Susannah and all enquireing friends your

[85] The supplies evidently failed to arrive, for the post was evau-
ated and burned about October 22, and the troops returned to Cap
au Gris.

[86] William Becknell was ensign in Callaway's company. He became a trader and made expeditions to Santa Fe in 1821 and 1823.
See his "Journal," in Missouri Historical Society, *Collections*, II,
55-67.

FORT JOHNSON, DRAWN BY CAPT. CALLAWAY

mother in particular tell her to keep Benj at home that he Cannot stand the fatieges of a Campaign I have had my health verry badly but at this Time am hearty but verry weak as for further particulars you will Learn from your Brother who will hand you this Letter. I Expect to see you in good Health if not in good situation and under those Hopes I Live and Remain your Loving and ever affectionate Husband

JAS. CALLAWAY

Mrs. Nancy Callaway

Camp Clemson
5th March 1815

Dear wife

I have Just Returned from Bests fort,[87] on yeastearday evening Mr. John Wheldon[88] and one of my men was up their and heare four or five Guns and saw two Indians they Returned to this place and we marched up to Mr Quicks[89] in order to save them families from the Tomohwak we arived thir after swimming wading and Traveling Through the mud and water untill about midnight this morning we went on to Bests Fort but the rain had put out all the sign we Returned to Camp where the Spies from Louter Creek say they saw the sign of six Horses and one footman I am Just a going to start after them

Your affectionate Husband

Nancy Callaway   JA^S CALLAWAY
    Crout Run
Capt. Wheldon

[87] Best's Fort was erected on the mainland near the western end of Loutre Island by Isaac Best in 1812.

[88] John Wheldon, in whose care this letter was sent, owned a large farm in what is now Dardenne Township, St. Charles county.

[89] Jacob Quick came from Germany and settled on the upper part of Loutre Island in 1811. He had married sons at this date.

DIARY

On the 22nd of august at twelve oclock we Left Cappo Grais with a fair wind this movement was agreeable to a Detachment order Read on parade the evening before we set out Lieut heampstead[90] was Directed to Reconniter ahead of the fleet Major Z. Taylor who commanded the party in front of the fleet Capt Rector next and Capt whitesides to bring up the Rear we set out with hearts elated and sails filled untill Near sunset and encamped on the west side.

23rd August set out at Day Light and in rowing One Mile we hoisted sails and Landed on an Isleand on the East side and breckfasted one hour & set sail at Nine oclock and sailed about three Hours and the wind fell went on & encamped on the west side.

24th August set out at half past four and passed the Mouth of Buflelow[91] and encamped in the Mouth of Nie in Disorder here a Number of the men ware readdy to feint with fateuge

25th set out and six men on Board of my Boats Took The Measles 10 others sick we Took a Narrow part of the River and the men have to wade and pull the Boats I am this Day verry unwell myself we encamped opposite high Bluffs below fort mason

26 August set out early and passed fort Mason at eight oclock and breakfasted at Lagotries old house where we regaled our selves on peaches I have become better more men have the Measles we passed

---

90 Stephen Hempstead of St. Charles county was appointed lieutenant of militia on June 4, 1812. Marshall, *Life and Letters of Frederick Bates*, II, 236.

91 Buffaloe creek, a small stream in Pike county, flows northeast into the Mississippi five miles below the mouth of Salt river.

the Bay Charles[92] and encamped on an Isleand Near the eastside

27 we set out early and Breakfasted where a perrara shuts in on the westside We send some Indians and whitemen to spy they Return immediately and Report no signs of Indians we encamped on an Isleand where the bloff shuts in on the river on the eastside

28th we started with full sails and breakfasted where a parara Shuts in on the westside and Set out at ten oclock with filled sheets which continue untill evening we passed the River wancondan[93] and arive at perara Del yar and Stayed all Night 29th we set out early and breakfasted on a willow beach we sent out spies the[y] Discover Indian sign and Return we pass a perara on the west side and encamp on the same side.

30th we set out early and pass a perra on the east side the first on that Shore my men becom verry sick at twelve oclock we entered the rapids and Lay all Knight in them.

31st we set out early and about breakfast the Majors Boat swung and broke his Steering oar I landed sent him mine and ten men he got to shore and mended his oar their sprung up a stiff Breese and arived at the head of the Rapids a beautiful perara on the west side and an old farm on the east side we traveled about Six miles and one of my men by the Name of Pointer Died and we encamped at fort Madison

[92] The Bay Charles was a projecting arm that extended northwest for several miles. It was located just east of Palmyra, Marion county.

[93] The Wyaconda, a considerable stream, flows southeast across Clark and Lewis counties and empties into the Mississippi at Lagrange.

1st of september thursday we buried the man and mended the mast that had been Carried away by a gale of wind from the Majors boat we set out with half filled sails the wind increased and we sailed about 10 miles and encamped on the east side untill 8 oclock and anchored out in the river for the first Time

2nd Sept Friday

we set out about Day Light and about ten we passed several pararas on the east side and some on the west we encamped on an Isleand Near the west side.

3rd Sept saturday

we set out and breakfasted on the same Isleand but in Runing along this moruning we Discovered a Dog after breakfast we passed high Land bluff barran on the east side and the Ioway River on the west under full sail which Lasted untill evening we landed got our Suppers and set sail and ran all Knight and breakfasted about 15 Miles below Rock River On the morning of the 4th we ran up to rock River Discovered Horese when we ware opposite the mouth we saw a Canoe of Indians they Ran ashore and two went up the river with the Canoe we Ran up and Landed about three mile above the river on an Isleand and got our supper the Indians built a Large fire on the main Land opposite to us in the morning of the 5th of Sept before Day the Indians commenced a fire on us wounded two of our men we peraded and Drove them off the Isleand two other men wounded in this action Capt Rector Droped Down a Small Distance below to prevent the Indians from Coming to our Isleand and about this time they commenced a Cannonnadeing on our Boats they over shot us at first but soon brought them to bear on us they shot one ball in the Commanding officers boat one through the spie Boat and

3 towards Capt allens boat one cut the steering oar off the Indians from all Quarters firing their Small armes at us and we Returned the fire from our Small arms and swivils for one hour when we ware obliged to Drop down as they fired from a battery and we from our boats We Dropt about 4 miles below and held a Council of war in which we concluded and it was best as they ware (as was supposed) five times our numbers & had as heavy mettle as us and acordingly it was so

MUSTER ROLLS, PAY ROLLS AND RECEIPT FOR ARMS

ROLL OF COMPANY OF CAVALRY—Undated.

James Callaway, Capt.
Prospect K. Robbins, Lieut.
James Whitesides, Ensign
Jonathan Riggs, Purser
Elisha Moore, 1st Seargt.
Larkin S. Callaway, 2nd Seargt.
Drury R. Prichet, 3rd Seargt.
William S. Williams, 4th Seargt.
Thomas Howell, Trumpeter
William Smith, Private
James Cleaver
Thomas Smith
John Stuart
James Deason
Robert Pruitt
Jacob C. Darst
Elijah Davis
William Jamerson
John Gibson
John M. Doff
John Deason

John Paterson
Gion Gibson
Thomas Witherinton
Willis Hensley
Thomas Cunegam
  [Cunningham]
Joseph Hanes [Hainds]
William F. Wells
Joseph Gibson
Wilfond Deason
Arthur Cordial
Ebenezer Davis
Evin Lemasters
Pierre Bergeron
Louis Pelleter
Antoine Mallet
Daniel Quick
James James
Philip Durton
D. Barton

MUSTER ROLL OF A COMPANY OF CAVALRY ACTING AS
MOUNTED RIFLE MEN COMMANDED BY CAPT. JAMES
CALLAWAY AND MUSTERED INTO SERVICE THE
29TH APRIL, 1813, AND CONTINUED IN SER-
VICE UNTIL THE 18TH MAY, 1813,
INCLUSIVE.

Names	Rank	When Mustered Into Service	To What Time Employed or Engaged
James Callaway	Capt.	29th April 1813	18th May 1813
Prospect K. Robbins	1st Lut.	" " "	" " "
John B. Stone	2nd L.	" " "	" " "
Jonathan Riggs	Cornet	" " "	" " "
Larkin S. Callaway	Sargt.	2nd May 1813	18th May 1813
John Baldridge	"	29th April 1813	" " "
William Smith	"	13th May 1813	" " "
Thomas Howell	Trumpt.	29th April 1813	18th May 1813
James Kerr	Private	29th April 1813	" " "
John Stuart	"	" " "	" " "
Francis McDermed	"	" " "	" " "
John Atkinson	"	" " "	" " "
Robert Pruit	"	" " "	" " "
Francis Howell	"	" " "	" " "
Joseph Hainds	"	" " "	" " "
Richard Barry	"	" " "	" " "
Thomas Smith	"	" " "	" " "
Adam Zumwalt 1st	"	" " "	" " "
Enock Taylor	"	" " "	" " "
Alexander Baldridge	"	" " "	" " "
Lewis Crow	"	" " "	" " "
Benjamin Howell	"	2nd May 1813	" " "
Antony C. Parmer	"	8th " "	" " "
Daniel Hays	"	13th " "	" " "
Boone Hays	"	13th " "	" " "
Adam Zumwalt 2nd	"	14th " "	" " "
John Howell	"	" " "	" " "

I certify on Honor that this Musterroll
exhibits a True and Correct Statement
of the Company of Cavalry under my Command.

(Signed)   James Callaway, Capt.

PAY TABLE

NOTES IN THE HANDS OF CAPT. CALLAWAY FOR COLLECTION.

By whom given	Amount	To whom given
Atkinson, John	$.50 cts.	James Callaway
" "	1.	" "
Breading, William	4.37½	" "
Crump, Daniel	11.75	" "
Emmons, A. Ira	33.	" "
Hubbard, Jabez	50	Lindsey Carson
Linville, Aaron	80	Joseph Gibson
Megill, John	4	James Callaway
Smith, William	35.	Joshua Dodson
Taylor, Zacheriah	150	Robert Cooper
Robertson, John	1.25	James Callaway
" "	3 6¼	" "
Price, Lemuel	32	Abram Darst

ROCK RIVER ACCOUNTS
ON MUSICKS COMPANY.

	Amount Due
Samuel Abbot	$4..11¾
Ignatius Anderson	6.. 7*½
Lindsey Burke	4..32
John Burnside	1..28¼
Philip Butler	..81
Johnathan Cottle	2..00¾
John Dozier	1..45
Peter Furlough	3..71½
John Howard	3..91½
John Jacobs	4..52¼
Page Johnston	..47½
Francois Mograin	..94¼
Jacob Noland	1..75
Jacob Trask	4.32
Johnathan Vess	2.87½
Caleb Witherington	3.24
Jobe Williams	1.01¼
Mel Whiteside	7.05½
Lieut. Williams	.40½

PAY TABLE CONTINUED

CALLAWAY'S COMPANY

	Amount Due
Ens. W. Becknell	7..46
Reese Bowen	1..54½
Nathan Coughman	3..03½
Joseph Collard	1..01¼
Daniel Crump	4..81
Hallard Dorcey	2. 97
Tract. Emmons	2. 46½
Aaron Gernsey	3. 44
Samuel Groshong	.94½
Lowrey T. Hampton	.98
Thomas Kerr	.33¾
James Lewis	2.95½
James Long	.36¾
Daniel Larrison	1.25
Joseph Mitchel	1.75½
F. McDermid	1.01¼
William Smith	1.62
William Woolf	4.45½
Lador Woods	12.64

CRAIG'S COMPANY

Jeremiah Able	1.35
John Brown	.60¾
James Brown	.40½
—— Bird	2.76¾
James Hamilton	1.28¼
—— Loyd	.40½
Nathane McCartie	.40½
—— Revah	1.98¾
John Sorrels	.47¼
Joshua Simpson	3.37½
Edward Stephenson	.64¼
Ebare Tayon	2.07½
John Wiggs	1.25
Louis Venice	.81

RECEIPT FOR ARMS

2nd March 1812   Saint Charles.

We the undersigned acknowledge to have received of Capt. James Callaway of the Cavalry of St. Charles one Sword and belt and one pistol arms of the United States which we severally promise to be accountable for and return when demanded by the said Capt. Callaway. Witness our hands the day and year above written.

Signed.	*Signed.*
X John B. Stone	Alexander Chambers
Jonathan Riggs,	John Howell,
Even Lemasters	Francis Howell,
Lewis Crow,	Larkin S. Callaway,
Thomas Howell,	Jacob C. Darst,
Elijah Davis,	Adam Zumwalt,
John Stewart	William Smith,
Joshua Dodson,	Joseph Haynes,
Daniel Hays,	Elisha Moore,
John Doff,	Lawry Hampton,
Anthony C. Parmers,	X Robert Pruett
Dury R. Rinhard	Joseph Gibson,
Thos. Smith,	James Gleasen
Thos. McNair,	John Deason,
Boon Hays,	James Deason,
Prospect K. Robbins	James Deason,
N. Howell X	Wilford Deason.

To said troop or any of its members which purser shall collect the same with all convenient speed and keep a correct account of all monies so collected by him and he shall keep the same subject to the orders and draughts of the * * * *

Receipts for public Armey.

THE CALLAWAY FAMILY

By Sarah Mercer Carpenter

The Callaway family is an ancient one and of English origin.[1] The name has many corruptions: Callowet, Callowe, Calloe, Killoway, Kullaway, and perhaps, though quite remotely Carroway and Galloway. It is probably of Anglo-Saxon origin as are so many with the "o" in the middle of the name.[1] The counties of Galloway in Scotland and Galway in Ireland lend some support to this theory. The fact that the Callaways unquestionably entered the Virginia gateway and did not come through William Penn's good city, as did so many of their eighteenth century associates and relatives in Virginia and Kentucky, points to the belief that they were primarily of English origin, although their attraction for the formality of the law and their frequent and lengthy discourses suggest Scotch and Irish influences.

In county Bucks, 1273, is found Walter Caleway. William Calleway in county Devon and Cassanda Caylleway in county Wilts. London Marriage Licenses, Vol. 1, p. 4, in 1524 William Caloway and Alice Cower, and among the baptisms recorded in Register of St. Columb, Mayor, p. 5 is Robert, son of John Calowie, 1549, Jane, daughter of Thomas Calwaye, 1554, p. 7, and Philip, son of Richard Callaway, 1683, p. 7.

[1] Bardsley, *Dictionary of English and Welsh Surnames*, 156; Phillmon, *Surnames*, 329; Barber, *British Family Names and Surnames*, 109; Harrison, *Surnames of the United Kingdom*, 66; Ferguson, *Teutonic Name System of France, England and Germany*, 437. See also Marshall, *Geneological Guide*, 452—Notes and Queries 1 ser. 7, 529-608. Hutchin, *Dorset*, 4, 194;— Berry, *Hampshire Genealogies*. Vivian, *Visitations of Devon;*—Weaver, *Visitations of Somerset (Keilway)*.

In Publications of the Huguenot Society and History of the Walloon Huguenot Church at Canterbury, Anglicized Names of the Foreign Settlers, 15, 216, the name is given as *Caloue*, meaning Callaway.

In the Somersetshire Visitations the following record of William Kelway seems of particular interest. The names of William, Thomas, and Richard appearing in counties Devon, Dorset, and Somerset offer as a possibility that part of England from whence came the Virginia Callaways.

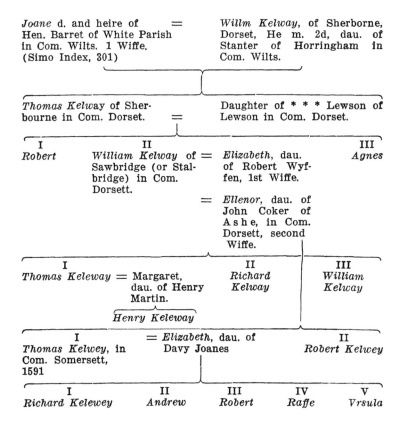

Joane d. and heire of Hen. Barret of White Parish in Com. Wilts. 1 Wiffe. (Simo Index, 301) = Willm Kelway, of Sherborne, Dorset, He m. 2d, dau. of Stanter of Horringham in Com. Wilts.

Thomas Kelway of Sherbourne in Com. Dorset. = Daughter of * * * Lewson of Lewson in Com. Dorset.

I Robert — II William Kelway of Sawbridge (or Stalbridge) in Com. Dorsett. = Elizabeth, dau. of Robert Wyffen, 1st Wiffe. = Ellenor, dau. of John Coker of Ashe, in Com. Dorsett, second Wiffe. — III Agnes

I Thomas Keleway = Margaret, dau. of Henry Martin. — II Richard Kelway — III William Kelway

Henry Keleway

I Thomas Kelwey, in Com. Somersett, 1591 = Elizabeth, dau. of Davy Joanes — II Robert Kelwey

I Richard Kelewey — II Andrew — III Robert — IV Raffe — V Vrsula

Weaver gives the arms of "Kelway of Stowford in Berwick, Somerset, as Ar. two glazier's snippers in Salture, Sa, between four pears, Or."

FIRST OF THE NAME IN AMERICA

In the "Lists of Living and Dead in Virginia, February 16, 1623" there is recorded among others at "James Cittie" one John Kullaway and at "Elizabeth Cittie," a Steven Calloe.

It is further recorded that Edmund Callaway[2] was transported in 1639 by William Barker in Charles City county and William Jones transported Step. Callowet in Northampton county in 1645. Steph Callowe was introduced into Lower Norfolk county by Thomas Gutheridge in 1652, and a William Calloway is noted as a witness to a deed in Surry county in 1654.[3]

In the Land office at Richmond, Virginia is the record of John King who received in 1642 a grant of 300 acres for the transportation into the Colony of six persons, namely: Anne, his wife, Katherine Kallway, Thomas Clay, Philip Neale, Alice Smith and Alice Cocke. A legend persists through notes of Callaway descendants that a Crown Grant gave 766 acres in Charles City county to Thomas Callaway in 1665 "for bringing sixteen persons into the colony." A thorough search, recently made, failed to establish this fact, unless it was recorded under the different variances of spelling.

It is quite possible that Edmund Callaway, of 1639, worked out his passage due to William Barker, and took up land of his own. It is further possible that Thomas and William may have been his sons and that Thomas with the characteristic Callaway energy had begun to develop and organize the county with his "sixteen persons" and his 766 acres. The vicissitudes of the Callaways during their sojourn in tidewater Virginia are indistinctly and meagerly recorded. The firebrands of Nathanial Bacon's prema-

[2] Greer, *Early Virginia Immigrants*, 57.
[3] *Tyler's Quarterly*, 2, 269.

ture rebellion threw into oblivion the records of James City and it is improbable that anything will ever come to light on this subject.

The trail is picked up again in Norfolk county in 1711 where "Elizabeth Callaway, widow woman" was then living.[4] A deed of gift indicates a daughter Suzanna Callaway and a son Thomas Burten, (the son was evidently by a former marriage).

The name is next found in Spotsylvania county, in 1732, where Thomas Callaway[5] signs as witness to a deed and again, in 1734, Thomas and William purchase land from David Williams.

There is no further record of this land in Spotsylvania county but may be found in Orange county which was formed from Spotsylvania in 1734. To identify the tidewater Callaways with those appearing in Caroline, Spotsylvania, Goochland, Albermarle, Brunswick, Lunenburg, Halifax and Bedford counties may always be a question of conjecture, and it is doubtful whether all the Callaways in America can be traced to a common ancestor as is so glibly done by many families when they pass into the haze that envelopes our American records before 1750.

Efforts to make a direct connection from the scattered notes and family traditions gathered here and there, with the Callaways in Caroline county, whose earliest records have also been destroyed, have met with continued failure. The most commonly accepted tradition of the family is that the original emigrant came from England to Virginia, and his descendants later settled in Caroline county. The facts brought out by historians and searchers point to this county as the first home of the ancestors of those who settled in southwest Virginia, Kentucky, and Missouri. They received large grants of land from Kings George

---

4 Norfolk County Deeds, 8, 86.
5 Spotsylvania County Deed Book A. 124 and Book B. 132.

the Second and Third, through the different governors, Lee, Dinwiddie, Fauquier, Dunmore, and others. Several thousand acres were granted to William, Richard, Francis and Thomas Callaway, who were according to the best authorities, brothers.

In a recent history of Campbell county,[6] the author has also failed to identify the elusive first emigrant, who may have been Joseph, Francis or William. Reference is made to Lyman C. Draper's Life of Boone and biographical sketch of Col. Richard Callaway of Bedford and Botetourt counties, Virginia, and later of Kentucky, which gives him as being the son of Joseph, and grandson of another Joseph, and this Joseph Callaway, Senior, as having emigrated from England. His son, Joseph Callaway, Junior, later settled in Caroline county, and was the father of seven sons and two daughters; Richard Callaway being the sixth son. Richard's parents and a brother died of fever within a short period, while he was still a youth. The remaining members of the family continued to live for several years in the old homestead, and, about 1740, settled in Brunswick county, which ultimately became Bedford county. The land grants are convincing proof of this statement.

CALLAWAY LAND GRANTS

The records in the Land Office at Richmond show grants of many thousands of acres to different members of the Callaway family under this form of spelling. The earliest is found in the year 1745, from George II to Francis Callaway for 400 acres in county of Goochland.[7] In 1747, he was granted a tract in Brunswick county; in 1759 another tract in Albemarle, and in 1761 still another grant of 375 acres in Bedford county. Grants totalling 15,565

---

[6] Early, *Campbell Chronicles and Family Sketches*, 358.

[7] *Land Grants*, 24, 40.

acres were made to William Callaway in the counties
of Brunswick, Lunenburg, Halifax and Bedford
covering a period from 1750 to 1772, most of which
land was in Bedford county after it was set off from
Lunenburg in 1754.

Richard Callaway received grants of 5785 acres
from 1754 to 1773 in Lunenburg, Bedford and Botetourt. Lesser grants were given to Thomas, James,
John and George Callaway in the counties of Halifax and Bedford between the years 1762 and 1763.
With this accumulation of vast sections of land they
early were classed among the landed gentry.

CALLAWAYS PROMINENT IN THE HISTORY OF BEDFORD
AND HALIFAX COUNTIES, VIRGINIA

The first of the Callaways to attain prominence
were William, Richard and Thomas. During the
French and Indian War they commanded frontier
forts, links in the chain that Washington and Dinwiddie established as a wall against Indian attack.
Richard and William rose to the rank of colonel of
militia by their unusual activity in this work, and
Thomas became Captain of Foot of the Halifax
county militia in the Indian war.

William Callaway, through his large land holdings
was appointed the first County Lieutenant in the
year 1754. "The County Lieutenant corresponded
to the Lord Lieutenant of England, and was one of
the most important men in the county. He received
his appointment from the Governor and the Council,
commanded the county militia, and was empowered
to place all male white persons, above the age of
eighteen, in the militia, and under such captains as
he wished to appoint. He could order private drills
whenever and wherever he pleased, and was under
compulsion to hold four general musters annually.
These musters constituted a distinctly social feature

. . . The County Lieutenant also presided over courts martial and exercised much authority in time of war."[8]

William Callaway was a member of the House of Burgesses, representing Bedford county from 1754 to 1758, and was also, one of the justices holding court in 1754, the earliest record of court held in the county. The Order Books of the Court show that he continued as a Justice of the County Court until the organization under the Revolution at the Convention of Virginia, July 3, 1775.

He founded the town of New London, the county seat of the New Bedford county in 1755, and the deed books record many transfers of property to his relatives and as inducements to people to locate in this village. It is possible the name was given to the town for reasons of sentiment, and for the locality of New London in Caroline county, the traditional and oft repeated place of birth of this branch of the Callaways.

He kept up his land acquisitions until 1774 by virtue of his services in colonial wars. He saw no active service in Lord Dunmore's war, but served in the mobilization of troops and gathering of supplies. He died intestate in the year 1777. James Callaway,[9] his eldest son and heir at law, qualified as his administrator. This colonial squire is worthy of more space than this article can afford him.

James Callaway was a member of the House of Burgesses for Bedford county from 1766 to 1769, and succeeded his father as County Lieutenant in 1778. He was a conspicuous and leading figure in this section during the Revolution. In 1781 he qualified as Commissioner of Peace and in 1785 was elected sheriff of the county. William Callaway, Jr.,

[8] Wingfield, *A History of Caroline County, Virginia*, 3.
[9] Bedford county Order Book, December Court, 1777.

son of the above William, also held offices of distinction and trust in the county, among them being that of County Lieutenant in 1782. He, too, bore the title of colonel, hence the records of father and son often may have been confused. John Callaway, the third son, qualified as captain in 1778; while Charles, the youngest son, received his commission as captain in 1781.

Francis Callaway, like his brothers, William, Sr., Richard, and Thomas, was also prominent in civil and military affairs. He was commissioned sheriff of Bedford county by King George, the Third, and one of the Justices of the County Court, which offices he held at the beginning of the Revolution. Later he is shown by deeds to be disposing of his landed interests before removing to Georgia where he founded the branch of the family that still exists in that state.

It is James Callaway, still another brother, who is the center of interest, and of whom little is known. The records of Bedford county show that he died intestate in the year 1773.[10] In September of that year an account of his estate was filed by the administrator, in which his widow, Mrs. Sarah Callaway, is mentioned. The record of this James may often have been confused with his nephew, Captain James Callaway, son of Col. William Callaway, Sr. However, the above named James and his wife, Sarah, were probably the parents of Flanders, John, James, Micajah and Edmund, and no doubt others. Mrs. Spraker[11] and other historians give the name of James as their father, and Col. Richard Callaway as their uncle.

With this historical background of the Virginia Callaways, it was quite natural that the adventurous

10 Will Book A 191, 197 Bedford county, Va.
11 Spraker, *The Boone Family*, 516.

members of the family should be among the first to join the advanced guard of civilization as it moved steadily westward.

Richard, the best known of the brothers, provides the link that carries this family on into Kentucky. With the characteristic restlessness of his race, he began to look around for new worlds to conquer as soon as his brother, William, effected the settled county structure of Bedford county. Not content to remain among his brothers and enjoy the prosperity that would have rewarded their colonization efforts, he traveled first to North Carolina, where the news of Henderson's settlement reached his ears, and then to Kentucky with Daniel Boone in 1775. He assisted in the founding of Boonesborough, was a member of the Transylvania Committee which met at that settlement, moved his daughters into the wilderness to grow up in that unsettled and savage community from whose dangers they narrowly escaped; was elected Burgess from Kentucky county in the first election of 1777; was Justice of the Peace; County Lieutenant; and Commissioner on the Cumberland road. He was placed in charge of the first ferry at Boonesborough and assumed many other honors and responsibilities parallel in nature to those of his older brother, William of Bedford county. It is not entirely out of line to suggest that William's position in the community became the ambition of Richard and it is partly for this reason that he sought new fields in order to attain the same offices.

In 1780 when he and others were engaged in the construction of his ferry boat, they were fired upon by a party of Shawnee Indians. Callaway was killed and scalped. Two days later his body was recovered and buried at a spot just back of the Fort. The County Court of Madison county, October 4, 1795, ordered to be recorded "that satisfactory proof being made to this Court the title to the ferry across the Kentucky river from Boonesborough to the opposite shore was vested and established in the name of the seven younger children of Richard Callaway.'"[12] Seven members of the Court were present and sitting.

Colonel Callaway was married twice and tradition seems sustained that his first wife was Frances, daughter of George Walton, of Bedford county, Virginia. From this marriage there were at least nine children, namely:

1. *Elizabeth,* known as Betsy, born in 1760. She with her sister, Frances, and Jemima Boone, were captured by the Indians. The story is too well known to be repeated here. She became the wife of Colonel Samuel Henderson just two weeks after she had been rescued, he being one of the rescue party.

2. *Frances,* born in 1762, married 1st, Colonel John Holder, who was also of the rescue party; and 2d, John McGuire.

3. *Lydia,* who married 1st, Christopher Irvine, b. Sept. 11, 1755, d. September 11, 1786, and from whom descends the late Governor David Rowland Francis. She married, secondly, General Richard Hickman.

4. *Eliza,* who married John Patrick.

5. *Sarah,* who married in September, 1761, Colonel Gabriel Penn of Amherst county, Virginia, son of Robert Penn and Mary Taylor.

6. *Molly* (Mary), became the wife of Charles Gwatkin, who was born in 1741 and died in 1791. They lived in Bedford county, Virginia.

7. *Nancy,* of Amherst county, as shown by deed of gift and power of attorney.

8. *George.*

9. *Caleb.*

[12] Madison county, Ky. Court Order Book B. 13.

By his second marriage with "the widow Hoy," whose maiden name was Elizabeth Jones, Colonel Callaway had three children: Richard, Jr., John and Keziah, who married Captain James French, as shown by deeds of gift, from their mother, Mrs. Elizabeth Callaway, widow of Richard Callaway recorded in Madison county, Kentucky, in 1796.[13] Several of the above named children are not mentioned in the will of Col. Callaway, dated Dec. 21, 1772. This will has been brought to light recently by Mr. Willard R. Jillson, where it was found recorded in Court of Appeals, Frankfort, Kentucky,[14] and is here published for the first time.

WILL OF RICHARD CALLAWAY

"In the name of God Amen, I Richard Callaway being low and weak but in perfect senses and memory and of Lawful mind of the morality of Life I do make this my last Will and Testament and first I give my soul to Almighty God who first Gave it to me and my body to the Earth to be Decently buried in a Christian like manner according to the discretion of my executors and as to my worldly goods I give and dispose of as follows. After all my just debts and funeral expenses are paid the remainder of my estate I dispose of as follows.

Imprimis I give and bequeath to my beloved Wife Elizabeth Callaway three negroes named Jane, Doll and Sall to dispose of as she sees cause at her death - I also give her one feather bed and furniture such as would be suttable for her. Also one Roane mare saddle and bridle these only I give during her life or widowhood.

Item I give and bequeath to my daughter Sarah Penn one Crown and no more. I also give and bequeath to my son George Callaway one Crown and no more. I also give to my daughter Molly Gwatkin one Crown and no more. My desire is that when my son Caleb Callaway comes of age that this tract of Land whereon I now live may be equally divided between him and my son Richard Callaway—Caleb Callaway having the part whereon my mill stands and quarter at present, my son Richard Callaway to have the other part when he comes of age.

My desire is that my executors may collect and pay all my just debts and I further desire they may sell as much of my stock as they think proper only leaving enough for my wife and children

[13] Madison county, Kentucky Deed Books D 142; F. 260, 281, 449.
[14] Deed Book J 9, 11.

that stays with her to subsist on. I further desire they sell all my Lands only the above mentioned Land that I am possessed with. I further desire that all my negroes may be kept together and my executors will endeavour to raise as much cash as will purchase this Land here joining me of Dowsons [Dawsons] and give my children such education as they think will suit them and when they come of age all to be equally divided amongst them.

Lastly I appoint Simon Miller, John Callaway and Charles Gwatkin executors of this my last Will and Testament. In witness whereof I have set my hand and seal this 21st day of December In the Year of Our Lord 1772.

(Signed)   RICHARD CALLAWAY.

Teste Chas. Gwatkin
       Thomas Brown
          his
       James X Taylor"
          mark

At a Supreme Court held for the District of Kentucky the 1st of March, 1784. This copy of the last Will and Testament of Richard Callaway deceased was produced in Court and ordered to be Recorded and on the motion of Caleb Callaway to be admitted to administration with the will annexed of said Deceased. Satisfactory proof was made to the Court that the Executors therein named had renounced their right of administration and Elizabeth Callaway, widow of said deceased having resigned her right of administration to the said Caleb Callaway. Thereupon administration is granted him he having executed and acknowledged Bond as the law directs.

Test John May, Clk.

With Colonel Richard, there went also his nephew, Flanders, who after the death of his own father, was lured by the adventurous life promised him by his uncle; Caleb, the son of Colonel Richard joined them in 1779. Then came James, Micajah, John and Edmund, all brothers of Flanders, and entries of thousands of acres were made by them. After the formation of the counties from Kentucky county, Virginia, their lands proved to be in Lincoln, Madison, Fayette, Bourbon, Jefferson and Nelson counties. Flanders resided principally in Fayette and Bourbon. In a deposition given before the Commissioners of Bourbon county in 1799 he gives his age as forty-seven, and tells of making improvements in company with Richard Callaway and Christopher Irvine, in 1776 and 1777, in the vicinity of Flat Lick on the branches of Hinkston Creek. Deeds in Fayette and Bourbon counties give evidence that he looked after the interests of his brothers, James and Micajah after they were captured by the Indians and held during the period of the Revolutionary War. By 1799 Flanders had disposed of most of his Kentucky lands preparatory to following his father-in-law, Daniel Boone, to Missouri, whose daughter, Jemima had become his wife soon after her return from captivity with Richard Callaway's daughters. In a power of attorney given to his brother, Edmund July 21, 1803, his residence is given as "of the District of Femozage in Louisiana County Mesoori,"[15] also in a deed the same year he is "of the Spanish Territory West of the Mississippi."[16] In this deed he conveys the last of his holdings to his brother James (who followed him a few years later to Missouri, settling in Howard County) and for whom, as well as his father, he named his eldest son —the brave Captain James Callaway. The following declaration of his brothers tell their own interesting stories.

DECLARATION OF JAMES CALLAWAY

STATE OF MISSOURI 〉
COUNTY OF HOWARD 〉 Ss.

On this tenth day of Oct. 1832 personally appeared before the Hon. David Todd, Judge of the Howard Circuit Court in the State of Mo., James Callaway a resident of Howard Co. Mo., aforesaid, aged about seventy-six years, who being first duly sworn according to law, doth, on his oath, make the following declaration, in order to obtain the benefit of the provision made by the Act of Congress, passed June

[15] Clark county, Ky. Deed Book 7. 56
[16] Circuit Court Deed Book A. 139, Fayette county, Kentucky.

7, 1832. That he enlisted in the army of the U. S. in the year 1777, with Capt. Henry Paulding, & served in the Regiment under the command of Col. John Bowman, of the Virginia State Line, and proceeded under them to Kentucky, for the purpose of defending the frontier settlements, at and near Boonesborough. He remained in the Service, under the officers aforesaid, for the term of six months, the period for which he entered service. When being stationed between thirty and forty miles from his Captain, and an opportunity offering to reenlist under Capt. Daniel Boone (since Col. Boon) he did so, neglecting to take any discharge from his former officer—in fact not deeming it of any importance in the then condition of the country. He remained stationed at Boonesborough under Col. Boone until about the first of Jan. 1778 when he was detailed among others, to proceed to the Blue Licks and make salt for curing provisions for the garrison. Here he remained employed until about the 8th of Feb. following, when the whole party with whom he was were taken by a party of Indians, and taken to their towns in Ohio (near where Chillicothe now stands) where, after remaining several days in consultation it was at last determned to send a portion of the prisoners (himself among the number) to Detroit, which they reached in May. Here, he understood he was purchased by the British Governor (Hamilton) and remained until November following, without having much to do except attend roll call every Sunday Morning. About this time he was employed by a resident merchant to go on service for him some distance, and being about to depart, was required before leaving, to take the oath of fidelity to his then Majesty George III. This he peremptorily refused to do, and was thereupon instantly put into prison and confined 14 or 15 days, when he was taken out, and sent under guard, and in Irons to Fort Niagara, where he remained in Irons and guarded about two weeks, and was thence placed on board a Ship and transported to Buch Island, thence placed on board a boat and sent to Montreal, where he remained about two weeks, and was then placed on board a Sloop (tied hand and foot) and sent to Quebec, where he was put in Jail, and kept there something like two years, when he was taken out and sent to St. Paul's Bay, which he reached in Oct. or Nov. in the year 1780. He remained here (a prisoner as aforesaid) about twelve months, when he was placed on board a ship, and sent round to New York. He was not landed however, but transferred to a "Cartel" and transplanted up the North River, to Dobbs Ferry, between thirty & forty miles above New York where he was either exchanged or parolled —he cannot say which—the only paper he received being a permit from an American officer (whose name he has forgotten) to go home, or wheresoever he pleased. He returned home to Bedford County in Virginia, the place where he was born in the year 1756, (or about that time, as he has no record of his age). It was in this county, also, that he resided when he entered the service as aforesaid—and having enlisted in the month of May (as he believes) 1777, and returned on the 24th day of Dec. 1781, he computes the whole period of his Service at four years and upwards of seven months.[17]

DECLARATION OF MICAJAH CALLAWAY

Washington County, Indiana,
Sept. 29, 1832.

About 74 years of age, entered the service of Revolutionary War as a volunteer in Botetourt county of Virginia, by joining a Company under Cap. Henry Paulding of Virginia Militia in April, 1777. The Company consisted of about 100 men. He marched with said company to Boonsborough, Kentucky and served nine months. He then volunteered under Col. Boon and in February, 1778, he was stationed at the Blue Lick with others making salt and whilst there he was taken with 26 others, Col. Boon among the number, by a company of Shawnee Indians of upwards of 100 and conveyed as a prisoner with the others to the Little Miami. James Callaway, Jesse Copper, Nat Bullock, John Holly, William Brooks and Samuel Brooks were among the number. He

[17] File W 9771, Pension Bureau, Washington.

remained a prisoner with the said tribe of Indians from that time for five years and five months during which time he moved with the tribe of Indians to different places in Ohio. After the tribe was driven from Little Miami by a party from Kentucky, it took its station on Mad River and remained there about one year, then moved up the Big Miami about twenty miles, remained sometime there, moved to a smaller stream emptying into the Miami and from that place the tribe was driven by a party under General George Rogers Clark, seven of the Indians being taken prisoners, the Queen of the Nation being away, (her name Lamalumgen), the tribe then took their station on St. Marys', remained there about three months. He was then employed as an Interpreter on behalf of said tribe to go to the Falls of the Ohio to treat on the subject of exchange of prisoners, seven Indians went with him to that place for that purpose. The exchange took place after he had been there about seven days. General Clark being there at that time and by whose assistance this declarant was released at that time. He was in some other places with said tribe during the time he was a prisoner which he cannot now particularly recollect, but he is positive he was a prisoner which as he has stated for about 5 years and five months during which time his suffering from stripes, hunger and cold, and the privations incident to a prisoner's life among savages are indescribable.

After his release he was variously employed in the service of his country in defending the frontiers against the Indians, he was a spy for General Wayne four months and was employed as interpreter in making a treaty at Limestone for the exchange of prisoners and also at the mouth of Big Miami, he acted as interpreter for General Sinclair and General Butler, that he has no documentary evidence and that he knows no person whose testimony he can procure who can testify as to his service.[18]

It is these later Callaways who assumed the principal roles in the development of Kentucky and Missouri, working out their destinies with only an

[18] File 17211, Pension Bureau, Washington, D. C.

occasional glimpse of fame to mark their pathway as fellow-toilers in the ranks of the great silent subordinate classes. No more representative pioneer can be found than Flanders Callaway, who though born in Virginia and for twenty-five years faced the difficulties of conquering the Kentucky wilderness, ended his life in Missouri in 1828, having lived all of his years in the most troublous and dangerous periods of our frontier through the very years when its struggles were at its height.

CALLAWAY MARRIAGES
Bedford County, Virginia

James Callaway—Sarah Tate, Nov. 24, 1756.

James Callaway—Elizabeth Early, daughter of Jeremiah, Sept. 22, 1777.

A letter written by James Callaway to the Clerk, James Steptoe, asking for marriage license to be issued, on account of business at the Iron Works he is unable to go to town to sign the bond, but would do so at first opportunity. This letter is filed with the Marriage Bond and dated Sept. 15, 1777.[19]

James Callaway and Mary ——— widow of Joseph Calland, before Dec. 15, 1800.[20]

The above shows the three marriages of Capt. James Callaway, son of Col. Wm. Callaway, Sr.

John Callaway—Tabitha Tate, March 29, 1758.

Charles Callaway—Judith Early, Widow Pate, Dec. 14, 1760 or 1768, daughter of Jeremiah Early and sister of Elizabeth, second wife of his brother, Capt. James Callaway.

Zachariah Callaway and Susanna Miller, daughter of Simon and Ann Miller, Dec. 14, 1774.[21]

Dudley Callaway—Patty Trent, Dec. 12, 1778, daughter Henry Trent.

James Callaway and Susan White, July 12, 1784, daughter of Stephen White (went to Kentucky and later settled in Howard County, Missouri. See Pension Bureau War Record and Declaration).

Charles Callaway, son of Wm. Sr., and Christianna Gallaway, daughter of John Gallaway, Feb. 24, 1785.

Joel Callaway and Lucy Abston, daughter of Jesse Abston, Dec. 24, 1793.

Canna Callaway and Bourne Price, daughter of Col. William Sr., Mar. 5, 1774.

[19] Bedford county Marriage Records.
[20] Cumberland county, Virginia—Deed Book 8, 408.
[21] Amherst county, Va. Marriage records.

Powhattan County, Virginia

Abner Early Callaway of Bedford county, and Ann Eliza Lewis, daughter of Francis Lewis, of Powhattan county, January 23, 1809.

William Callaway and Ann Crump, daughter of Richard Crump, Oct. 28, 1807.

Kentucky

Anne Callaway—Robert Graham, Jan. 21, 1813, Bourbon county.

Charity Callaway—William Collier, Feb. 14, 1805, Jefferson county.

Charles Callaway—Elizabeth Eubank, Jan. 24, 1811, Clark county.

Chester Callaway—Elizabeth Gilbert, Oct. 24, 1809, Ohio county.

Clement Callaway—Pamelia Groomes, Aug. 1, 1825, Bourbon county.

Edmund Callaway—Athaliah Wright, April 2, 1798, Bourbon county.

Elizabeth Callaway—Charles B. Clark, daughter of Edmund Callaway (above) whose will is recorded in Christian county, Book C. 554.

Elizabeth Callaway—Samuel Henderson, Oct. 7, 1776, Kentucky county.

Elizabeth Callaway—James Robison, Nov. 22, 1812, Jefferson county.

Elizabeth Callaway—Robert Graham, Dec. 3, 1813, Bourbon county.

Frances Callaway—Elijah Crowe, Jan. 21, 1811, Ohio county.

Henry Callaway—Ann Shearman, Feb. 7, 1828, Bourbon county.

James J. Callaway—Catherine Carneall, June 1, 1815, Shelby county.

James Callaway—Mehala Mills, Mar. 23, 1823, Ohio county.

John Callaway—Marthy Robertson Booker, no date, probably 1807, Clark county.

John Callaway—Milly Callaway, Feb. 28, 1814, Clark county.

Kesiah Callaway—James French, June 19, 1783, Lincoln county.

Lewcy Callaway—James Irwin, Aug. 1, 1821, Christian county.

Mary Ann Callaway—Edward Payne, Sept. 15, 1826, Christian county.

Micajoah Callaway—Frances Hawkins, April 4, 1805, Garrard county.

Rachel Callaway—George Shaler, Mar. 3, 1795, Jefferson county.

Richard Callaway—Margaret Wells, Nov. 25, 1790, Madison county.

Richard Callaway—Ann Crawford, July 13, 1820, Shelby county.

Sarah Callaway—Robert Tarlton, Feb. 10, 1810, Ohio county.

Sarah Callaway—Francis Forbes, Feb. 12, 1799, Jefferson county.

Sarah Callaway—John Cheetham (daughter of Edmund) Christian county.

Samuel T. Callaway—Mary A. Means, June 6, 1800, Christian county.

Stephen Callaway—Sally Bryan, Oct. 10, 1810, Jefferson county.

Tonzay Callaway—William Summers, June, 1820, Ohio county.

Thomas Callaway—Ann Elizabeth Smith, Mar. 22, 1819, Jefferson county.

Thomas H. Callaway—Susan Daniel, April 22, 1822, Christian county.

William Callaway—Mille Eubank, Jan. 1, 1802, Clark county.

William Callaway—Rebecca Williams, June 2, 1836, Ohio county.

Zachariah Callaway—Phebe Cleaver, Feb. 17, 1805, Jefferson county.

NOTES

EHXIBIT OF MEDALS AND TROPHIES BESTOWED ON

COLONEL CHARLES A. LINDBERGH

(Honorary Member of the Missouri Historical Society)[1]

The decorations and trophies bestowed by individuals and nations upon Colonel Charles A. Lindbergh, in recognition of his daring non-stop flight from New York to Paris, were placed on exhibition by the Missouri Historical Society in the Jefferson Memorial on June 25th, for a period of ten days.

Approximately 80,000 people visited the Museum during that time. Colonel Lindbergh called one evening at eight o'clock to see his collection, much of which he had not seen before. On being told that the crowds continued to come in as large numbers as on the opening days, he expressed the wish that the collection be kept on display by the Missouri Historical Society for an indefinite period.

Some of the most important articles are:

The United States Distinguished Flying Cross conferred by President Coolidge. The first one ever presented.

British Distinguished Flying Cross

Cross of the French Legion of Honor. In addition to the one conferred upon him by the French Government, Col. Lindbergh was given two additional ones. The first, in miniature, which decorated the coat of one of Marshal Foch's Aides, was transferred to Lindbergh's coat. The second Cross, which had been conferred upon the Captain of a French Liner during the War, was given by him, to Colonel Lindbergh, in New York.

Cross of the Order of Leopold (Belgium)

King Albert Medal (Belgium)

Medal from Marshall Foch and the "Comité de l'Union Interalliée"

[1] The grateful thanks of the Society are here given to Mr. Reid Jones for installing the Exhibit.

LINDBERGH DECORATIONS AND TROPHIES

1. Gold Medal—N. Y. Police Dept.
2. Fr. Legion of Honor.
3. Miniature Legion of Honor presented by Foch's Aide who was wearing it.
4. Belgian Order of Leopold.
5. British Distinguished Flying Cross.
6. U. S. Distinguished Flying Cross.
7. R. Orteig (donor) Prize Medal—Gold.
8. Silver Medal—N. Y. State "For Valor."
9. Hospitaliers Sauveteurs.
10. Special Gold Medal—Albert of Belgians.
11. Gold Key & Badge—City of Paris.
12. Lapel Button—Ligue Internatl. Aviateurs.
13. Gold Key—City of London (small).
15. Gold Medal—School Children of Brooklyn, N. Y.
16. Flying Chevron.
17. Special Gold Medal—U. S. Veterans of Foreign Wars.
18. Miniature Brit. Fr. & Belg. Medals for Civilian Dress.
19. Gold & Enamel St. Christopher's Medal—for plane.
20. Silver St. Christopher's Medal.
21. Gold Medal—City of N. Y.—Mayor's Reception.

© 1927

Medal and Badge from The Lafayette Escadrille

Cross of the "Société des Hospitaliers Sauveteurs" (French Red Cross)

Other crosses and medals conferred by the following:

Aeronautical Chamber of Commerce of America

Aero Club of France

Aero Club of Belgium

Raymond Orteig Prize Medal

U. S. Flag Association

U. S. Veterans of Foreign Wars

Spanish War Veterans

Clemenceau War Orphans

Alsace

City of Paris

City of New York

City of St. Louis

Chamber of Commerce of Valenciennes

Police Department of New York

Mayor's Reception Committee of New York

New York State "Par Valor"

Nungesser Medal

School Children of New York

Gold keys to the City of London

Gold key to the City of Paris

Gold Box and Script from the City of St. Louis

2 Silver Globes, Terrestrial and Celestial Spheres. Made about the year 1700. Presented by W. R. Hearst of New York.

From Louis Bleriot, a fragment of the propeller from his plane in which he made the first flight across the English Channel.

Fragment from plane of famous French Ace, Pegoud, who was the first to fly up-side-down. He was killed in 1915.

Framed testimonial to Col. Lindbergh, from churches of all sects in New York City

Colonel's Commission from Missouri National Guards

Colonel's Commission from U. S. A. Air Reserve Corps

Rating Certificate, Air Corps Reserve

International Pilot's License

Testimonials signed by famous aviators

Gold Loving Cup, from London Daily Mail, which inaugurated the first Trans-Atlantic flight

Resolutions adopted by City Council of Sacramento designating "Lindbergh Field"

Gold Thermos Bottle, from U. S. Secretary of the Navy, Secretary of War and Secretary of Commerce

Gold Life Membership Card from National Association Professional Baseball League

Emblem, National Baseball League, showing Spirit of St. Louis on top of baseball, in gold

Gold Pass from National Baseball League

Gold and Diamond Pass from Shubert Theatre Corporation

Water Canteen, part of Lindbergh's equipment on flight

Chart used by Lindbergh during his flight

Condensing Flask, carried in case of emergency. If one is forced into the sea without drinking water the flask may be immersed into the sea, and by breathing into the flask, the rapid evaporation causes the breath to condense into sufficient moisture to prevent one's dying of thirst.

Several Air Mail Letters of enormous size, autographed by air mail pilots from various sections of the country, are among the exhibits.

Also, several watches, diamond stick pins, linkbuttons, jeweled fountain pens, jeweled money clasp, Air-plane fire-extinguishers, pipes, radiator ornaments, books, paintings, cigars, binoculars, goggles, etc, etc.

A document highly prized by Colonel Lindbergh, shows a number of autographs, surrounding a water color sketch of the head of an American Indian Chief. Soon after the definite organization of the Lafayette Escadrille in 1916, the pilots of this brilliant flying squadron, met one evening to select an insignia or emblem for their planes. Of those submitted, the one by Hinkle, was adopted. Captain Verdy, who was in command of Group P. S., at the time, suggested that all members present should autograph the drawing. A few days later, the American escadrille lost three of her pilots, who died in

LINDBERGH DECORATIONS AND TROPHIES

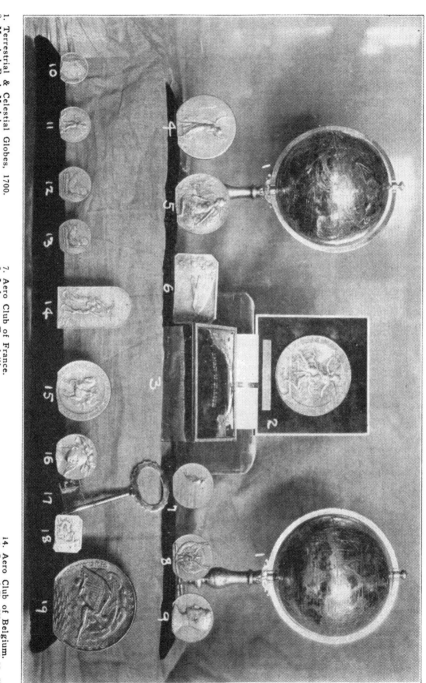

1. Terrestial & Celestial Globes, 1700.
2. Marshal Foch Medal.
3. St. Louis Gold Box and Scroll.
4. St. Louis Medal.
5. Paris.
6. Aeronautical Chamber of Commerce of Amer.

7. Aero Club of France.
8. Lafayette Escadrille.
9. Willy Coppens.
10. Napoleon 5 franc piece, 1813.
11. Brussels.
12.-13. Clemenceau War Orphans.

14. Aero Club of Belgium.
15. Soc. of Fr. Women of N. Y.
16. Alsace.
17. Key to London.
18. Valenciennes.
19. New York City.

action, and these were followed by the deaths of de Laage, Lufberry, Hurrit and others. This relic, carefully preserved by Captain Verdy, was sent by him to Colonel Lindbergh, through Ambassador Herrick, with the following letter:

Paris, May 24, 1927.

Mr. Ambassador:

I take great pleasure in asking your Excellency to have the kindness to do me the great favor of presenting this modest souvenir to your glorious and sublime aviator, Charles A. Lindbergh.

Being an aviator myself, one of the most obscure ones, I do not know how to express my admiration for his tremendous feat, so, *I offer him one of the most precious souvenirs, which I have kept, of the Great War, 1914-1918.* ◆

His brothers of the Lafayette Escadrille came first to help us in the gigantic fight for Right and Liberty, and gave their blood for us. He, Lindbergh, came today to bring us greeting from our brothers of American Aviation, among whom I have so many friends; it is the "trait d'union" between these two countries.

May he guard carefully, the signatures of these dead heroes and may he recognize in this act of offering him this souvenir, the desire I have of placing it in the hands of the most glorious of our heroes of the air.

Thanking your Excellency, I beg to remain,

Most respectfully,

B. VERDY.

For the benefit of those who are away for the summer, as well as for the visitors who will attend our fall festivities, it is probable that the Lindbergh exhibit will be kept open until the end of October.

NETTIE H. BEAUREGARD,
Archivist and Curator.

QUERIES

1. ADAMS-PREWITT. Who were the parents of Michael Prewitt, and did he or his father have Colonial service? Who were the parents of Elizabeth Adams, wife of Michael Prewitt, and cousin of John Adams, president of the United States?

2. MOSS-TOMLINSON. Names of parents of Frederick Moss, and Colonial service wanted. Names of parents of Sally Tomlinson, wife of Frederick Moss; also colonial service desired.

3. MARTIN-MIMS. Wanted names of parents of Melly Ann Martin who married Thomas Mims, Jr., February 10, 1698, in Goochland county, Virginia; also colonial service of David Mims, of Goochland county, Virginia, born in 1700.

4. WELDY or WILDY. Colonial service wanted of William Weldy or Wildy, whose will is recorded in Deed Book 5, 130, Goochland county, Virginia; also name of his wife.

5. RIDDLE. Who were the parents of Thomas Riddle of Goochland county, Virginia? He received a grant of land, May 20, 1764.

> Mrs. Wallace Delafield,
> 5026 Westminster Place,
> St. Louis, Mo.

6. WILLIAMS-BUTLER. Wanted ancestry of Edmund Williams of North Carolina and Watauga Settlement. He served on the Committee of Safety, and married Lucretia ———, said to be related to President Adams' family. Their daughter, Lavinia Williams married, in 1795, Jonathan Tipton *III*, who was the youngest of nine sons of Col. John Tipton, sheriff of North Carolina. Col. Tipton, born 1732, Shenandoah Valley, Virginia, died Aug., 1813, married, 1753, Mary Butler. This Butler connection is also wanted.

7. WEAR or WEIR-GILLILAND. Col. Samuel Wear or Weir of Virginia, moved to Watauga settlement, was associated with Gov. Sevier, and said to have been related to him. He married, 1st, Mary Thompson, 2d, Mary Gilliland. Proof that she was the daughter of John Gilliland of King's Mountain fame wanted.

8. MERRITT-WHEATON. Ancestry wanted of Merritts of Southwest Virginia, Holston river country. In about 1780 moved from Virginia to South Carolina, Greenville District. Benjamin Merritt married, in Virginia, in 1773, Eleanor Wheaton. Their son, Wheaton Merritt, b. Feb. 2, 1774, married, Feb. 25, 1796, Sarah Barton, b. April 16, 1775. Wanted, also, names of ancestors of Eleanor Wheaton. The daughter of Wheaton Merritt and Sarah Barton, Narcissa Ragsdale Merritt, b. 1805; d. May 15, 1845, married, Dec. 28, 1824, Ezekiel James Salmon, b. July 5, 1798, Greenville District, S. C., d. Sept. 15, 1851; both buried in Versailles, Morgan county, Missouri.

9. BARTON-W I L L I A M S O N. Thomas Barton, Greenville District, S. C. had three brothers: Benjamin, of Pendleton, S. C., (who had son called Thomas, Jr.); William, of Spartansburg, and David of Greenville (who m. Nancy Barrett and had nine children. I have names of these). Thomas Barton m. Bethia Williamson. Wish to get names of parents of both. Their children were: David, m. Nancy Rutherford; Rebecca, m. Arthur Barrett; Sarah, or Sally, m. Wheaton Merritt; William, m. 1st. Charlotte Anderson, 2d. Stocky Pryor; John, never married; Elizabeth, m. 1st. Wm. Rutherford, 2d. William Young, 3d. Rolland Suggs; Benjamin, never married; Elisha m. Luson Bradley and died in Alabama; Thomas, m. Rebecca Plumbly.

MRS. HOWARD BAILEY,
4944 Lindell Blvd.,
St. Louis, Mo.

CPSIA information can be obtained
at www.ICGtesting.com
Printed in the USA
LVHW022109270219
608942LV00019B/1349